A. ROSENBLATT,
prop.

John Trumbull's 1792 portrait of Alexander Hamilton,
Courtesy Credit Suisse First Boston, New York

PRACTICAL PROCEEDINGS

IN THE SUPREME COURT

OF THE STATE OF NEW YORK

*Hamilton's
Practice Manual*

◆ ◆ ◆

Alexander Hamilton

2004

New York Law Journal

Jacket Design: *Michael Ng*

Interior Page Design & Production: *Amparo Graf*

Library of Congress Cataloging-in-Publication Data

Hamilton, Alexander, 1757-1804.
      Practical proceedings in the Supreme Court of the State of New York / by Alexander Hamilton, with foreword by Willard Sterne Randall, Julius Goebel, Jr.
          p. cm.
ISBN 1-58852-128-1 (hardcover : alk. paper)
1. Civil procedure—New York (State)—Early works to 1800. 2. New York (State). Supreme Court—Early works to 1800. I. New York (State). Supreme Court. II. Title.
      KFN5995.H36 2004
      347.747'035—dc22   2004013805

CONTENTS

Preface   vii

Foreword   ix

Introduction to Hamilton's Practice Manual   1

Practical Proceedings.   21

Exhibits   107

PREFACE

This edition of Alexander Hamilton's practice manual for the New York Supreme Court presents a detailed look at the state's courts at the end of the Revolutionary War from one of the giants of early American history. Hamilton wrote it in the waning years of the eighteenth century as a study guide while he was cramming to pass the bar, and it became a valuable reference for New York lawyers for years after. We at the New York Law Journal decided to reprint the manual because we felt that it is likely to be of interest to judges, lawyers and history buffs in that it portrays early American law practice in all of its sophistication and complexity.

The inspiration for this book, published 200 years after Hamilton's death following his duel with Aaron Burr, came from the captivating biography of Hamilton written by Willard Sterne Randall, *Alexander Hamilton: A Life* (2003). I would like to thank Professor Randall, who was gracious enough to write a foreword to the practice manual, putting it in perspective in the context of Hamilton's life and work.

I would also like to thank Columbia University Press for allowing us to reprint its 1964 scholarly edition of Hamilton's manual, along with the footnotes and introduction that accompanied it in the first volume of the five-volume *The Law Practice of Alexander Hamilton: Documents and Commentary,* edited by Julius Goebel, Jr.

And finally, Credit Suisse First Boston deserves thanks for allowing us to reprint the beautiful portrait of Hamilton seen on the book's cover. The portrait hangs in the hallway of Credit Suisse's building on Park Avenue South in Manhattan.

Rex Bossert   July 2004
Managing Editor, *New York Law Journal*
(now Editor-in-Chief, *The National Law Journal*)

FOREWORD

by Willard Sterne Randall*

If we know anything at all about Alexander Hamilton, it is probably little more than three things. His face is on the ten dollar bill. He was the first Secretary of the Treasury. He died in a duel with Aaron Burr. Beyond that, especially if we have taken a history lesson from his archrival, John Adams, Alexander Hamilton was "the bastard brat of a Scots peddler." The truth about Alexander Hamilton is much more fascinating than the durable slur of a political enemy.

....

* Willard Sterne Randall is the author of twelve books, including five biographies and two biographical readers. A former investigative reporter, he received the National Magazine Award for Public Service from Columbia Graduate School of Journalism, the Hillman Prize, the Loeb Award and three Pulitzer Prize nominations during his seventeen-year journalism career in Philadelphia. After graduate studies in history at Princeton University, he turned to writing biographies. His first, *Benjamin Franklin and His Son,* won a Frank Luther Mott Award for research from University of Missouri Graduate School of Journalism. *Benedict Arnold, Patriot and Traitor,* was a finalist for the Pulitzer Prize and runner-up for the Los Angeles Times Book Prize. *Thomas Jefferson, A Life,* was also nominated for the Pulitzer Prize and was selected as one of Publishers Weekly's best biographies of 1993. *George Washington, A Life,* was included in Readers Digest's Best Nonfiction of 1997. Randall recently received the Award of Merit from the American Revolution Roundtable in New York City, only awarded twice before in that organization's 45-year history. His latest biography, *Alexander Hamilton, A Life,* was published by HarperCollins in January, 2003. He has co-authored four books with his wife, the poet Nancy Nahra, including *American Lives,* a two volume collection of short biographies that has been used in more than 100 colleges and universities. A contributing author to *MHQ: The Quarterly Journal of Military History,* he regularly reviews biographies for *New York Newsday* and the *Journal of American History.*

Hamilton was born January 11, 1755, in the British colony of Nevis, in the Caribbean. His mother, Rachel Fawcett, daughter of a Huguenot refugee, was married at sixteen to Johann Levine, a much older German Jewish merchant-planter. He thought she had money; her mother thought he did. As he ran through her dowry and went ever deeper into debt, Levine abused Rachel. They had a child, Peter, but Levine had Rachel imprisoned for refusing his connubial rights. She fled to her family on the Danish island of St. Croix. About three years later, Rachel began a common-law relationship with James Hamilton, impecunious fourth son of a wealthy Scottish laird. Under the English law of primogeniture and entail, only the first-born inherited. James was relegated to serving an apprenticeship in a Glasgow linen trading firm, then sailed for the Caribbean just as the linen market collapsed. Social slippage was the fate of many aristocrats, who had only their pretensions left while they worked as traders and plantation managers.

Drifting from island to island, the Hamiltons, as they signed themselves when standing up for others in Anglican church services, had two sons. The elder, Alexander, was nine when his parents learned that, after a twelve-year separation, Rachel's first husband, intending to remarry, had divorced her under Danish law on grounds of adultery and desertion. Under Danish law, he could divorce her; under English law, she could not divorce. Under Danish law, he could remarry; under Danish law, she could not. James Hamilton sailed away, sparing his wife a charge of bigamy. From that day on, Alexander Hamilton was considered a bastard. He never saw his father again.

Rachel opened a dry goods business in St. Croix, where Alexander worked after days in a school run by a Jewish mistress: illegitimate, he was barred from the island's Calvinist schools. In school, he learned a little Hebrew; from his mother he learned fluent French. When Alexander was thirteen, Rachel died of yellow fever. Her first husband seized her estate. Alexander's meager inheritance went to Peter Levine, the half-brother he had never met. A penniless orphan, Alexander was apprenticed as a clerk to a trading firm in St. Croix. He learned quickly. He was only seventeen when his boss had to go home to New York on sick leave, putting his young assistant in charge. For six months, Hamilton gave orders to ships' captains, mapped out voyages, rejected shoddy goods, learned all about cargo, foreign exchange and smuggling, knowledge he turned on its head when he became the first United States Collector of the Port of New York after the Revolution and then, as Secretary of the Treasury, founded the Customs Service and the Coast Guard.

Rewarded with a scholarship to study in mainland British America, Hamilton attended Elizabethtown Academy in New Jersey, brushing up his Latin and Greek before applying to the College of New Jersey (now Princeton). Refused because he insisted on accelerated study, he matriculated instead at King's College (now Columbia) in New York. In the college's library, he read international law, including Blackstone, Locke, Pufendorf, Vattel and Grotius, and the classics, writing unsigned Revolutionary pamphlets in his dormitory room by candlelight at night. He was poor at math, this future first Secretary of the Treasury. He flunked it and failed pre-med.

When the Revolution began, Hamilton converted his literary discussion club into an artillery company, the Fifth Company of the First Regiment, the oldest surviving unit of the U.S. Army. He stole twenty-one British cannon from the battery at Fort George while under fire from the man-of-war *Asia*. Hamilton took revolution seriously. One of the few high-ranking officers *not* from a leading American family, he espoused equality. He insisted that a veteran sergeant be promoted to lieutenant; he crusaded for better rations, fatigue uniforms, good shoes for his men. He lobbied New York's Provincial Congress for parity in pay between militia and Continental soldiers.

Assigned to build a fort at Canal Street in what is today's Greenwich Village, the twenty-one-year-old Hamilton, now a Continental Army captain, watched the British invasion of New York City through a spyglass. After the Americans were routed at Brooklyn Heights, Hamilton sent an escape plan to George Washington that saved his army. Hamilton himself narrowly escaped, guided to safety up Bloomingdale Road by Captain Aaron Burr. With only two cannon left, Hamilton repeatedly held off British attacks while Washington's tattered army fled across to New Jersey. When Washington sent an aide to see who was shielding his rear, the veteran "noticed a youth, a mere stripling, small, slender, almost delicate in form, marching with a cocked hat pulled down over his eyes, apparently lost in thought, with his hand resting on a cannon, every now and then patting it, as if it were a pet." Washington personally witnessed Hamilton's valor at the Battle of Trenton, promoted him to lieutenant-colonel and made him his aide-de-camp, a post Hamilton held for four years.

Given charge of prisoner-of-war exchanges, negotiations and espionage. Hamilton funneled information from some 220 operatives behind British lines in New York. He put his French to use as translator and liaison to the French army and navy. With Baron Steuben, he reformed and retrained the army at Valley Forge. He wrote the infantry training manual of arms still in use. Fiercely loyal to Washington, Hamilton uncovered the Conway Cabal, a plot aimed at displacing Washington as commander in chief. Washington eventually rewarded Hamilton by giving him his own light infantry battalion. Hamilton personally led the last crucial charge of the Revolution, capturing Redoubt Number Ten at Yorktown.

Hamilton the war hero married into a land-rich, politically prominent Hudson Valley family, the Schuylers, and set his cap at a career combining government and the law. On January 18, 1782, the New York Assembly passed a law suspending until the last day of

April 1782 the 1778 requirement of a rigorous three-year clerkship for "such young gentlemen who had directed their studies to the profession of the law but upon the breaking out of the present war had entered the army." Hamilton moved to Albany and began to read law in the office of James Duane, mayor of New York City and a specialist in land law. Hamilton's first legal filing was to seek a six-month extension for his studies. He succeeded along with only one other applicant, Aaron Burr. Hamilton's bold request came only eleven days after his appointment as the federal tax collector for the state of New York. The appointment stemmed from a series of his letters to members of Congress and *The Continentalist* newspaper articles he had published while still in the army. Hamilton characteristically juggled his six-month crash course of law studies with his first political office.

To synthesize the vast amount of material, he found there was no manual of proper legal procedures to expedite his studies. So Hamilton wrote one, the first handbook for the use of practicing lawyers ever written in America. He summarized proper procedures and the essence of the laws in a 177-page manuscript of some 40,000 words under major headings such as Damages, Process, Joint Actions, Judgment and Execution, Pleas, Venue and Habeas Corpus. According to Julius Goebel, pre-eminent authority on Hamilton's legal career, so accurate and thorough was his research that modern legal scholars have found only eight minor errors in the work. Hamilton's book, the only legal handbook available for law students struggling with the transition from English to American law, has a wry, resigned, almost sarcastic tone perfect for its audience. Hamilton criticized the inconsistency of New York court pleadings as "among the absurdities with which the law abounds." One section of common law, on trespass and ejectment, he derided as "a creature of Westminster Hall (that) subsists chiefly upon fiction." Subsequently published, Hamilton's lawbook became the standard manual for New

York lawyers and was used for decades. While Hamilton disparaged "cavilling" lawyers and privately called the practice of law "the art of fleecing neighbors," he loved the law.

As a practising lawyer, Hamilton quickly rose to the top rank of New York lawyers (there were only thirty-five lawyers in New York City when he hung out his shingle on Maiden Lane). His most important civil case, *Rutgers v. Waddington,* pitted the fragile young American democracy against international law. Under New York's Trespass Act of 1783, defendants were prohibited from pleading that they had acted under orders of the occupying British. Contradicting international law, the act also denied defendants the right to appeal to a higher court. The act contravened the very peace treaty that granted American independence.

Hamilton, now a delegate to the Continental Congress, decided to take the suit of a widow, Elizabeth Rutgers, against two Loyalists who had improved her abandoned brewery and made a fortune slaking British thirst. Hamilton, for the first time arguing the principle of judicial review, told the Mayor's Court that the state law violated the law of nations and the mandate of Congress. He argued that international treaties must be considered the law of the United States. He prevailed, Mayor Duane carefully adding in his ruling that the case stopped short of establishing a precedent of judicial review, "for this were to set the judicial above the legislature." Between 1784 and 1791, Hamilton defended some forty-four Loyalists prosecuted under the Trespass Act and twenty Loyalists prosecuted under New York's Confiscation Act. His efforts made New York the first state to re-established the civil rights of Loyalists after the Revolution. In Congress and in court, Hamilton, emerging as New York's preeminent marine lawyer, became the advocate of commercial interests.

Hamilton's career as a public official is well known. A delegate to the Constitutional Convention of 1787, in his only speech he lectured the Founders for six hours on the need for a strong national government under a president kept in check only by powers divided under three branches, executive, legislative and judicial. Except for presidential tenure, his plan closely resembled the final outline of the new Constitution. Setting aside his law business for nearly a year, to help influence ratification in New York, he wrote fifty-six of the eighty-five Federalist Papers, generally regarded as the greatest commentary on the Constitution and federalism ever written. Then he led the fight for ratification in the New York Assembly.

Once New York ratified, Hamilton was eligible to serve in the new national government. On September 11, 1789, President Washington appointed Hamilton the first Secretary of the Treasury, giving him 120 days to come up with a plan for eliminating staggering state and national Revolutionary War debts. In a series of four "Reports" to Congress, Hamilton proposed creating a national debt that would assume all war debts and pay them at par. To facilitate this, he urged establishing a national bank; the first American corporation; a mint to mill a decimal currency; and a sinking fund to retire the debts with revenues from customs duties and the sale of government bonds. Attracting foreign investors, Hamilton's "blessing" was immediately successful. Yet Hamilton came into conflict with Secretary of State Thomas Jefferson and with Speaker of the House James Madison, Hamilton's co-author of the Federalist Papers; this pointed to the rift that created two political parties, an eventuality not foreseen in the Constitution. Hamilton never understood Jefferson's enmity, which stemmed from the Virginian's belief that Hamilton was scheming to erect an American version of the British system. The result was that Hamilton emerged as the leader of the Federalist Party, forerunner of today's Republican Party, and Jefferson as leader of the Democratic-Republicans, which became the Democratic Party.

Father of seven children, Hamilton was constantly in debt during his government years. He officially retired from public life in 1795 and returned to his New York law practice, where he worked long hours as one of New York's two leading lawyers. The other was Aaron Burr, often Hamilton's co-counsel and increasingly his rival for control of New York politics. Hamilton emerged on the national stage once more during the "Quasi-War" with France when Washington would only agree to resume his duties as commander-in-chief if Hamilton were his second in command. Hamilton proudly assumed the rank of major general and acted as Inspector General of the Army, building up America's defenses during the Napoleonic Wars.

Hamilton's last celebrated court case was to have lasting importance. In February, 1804, only five months before he died in a duel with Burr over an insult, Hamilton traveled to Albany to appeal the libel conviction of an upstate printer, Harry Croswell, who had written that now-President Jefferson had paid the scurrilous pamphleteer James Thompson Callender to defame Washington and Adams. Under English common law, truth was not a defense. To a packed courtroom, Hamilton delivered one of his most brilliant speeches. Only truth could stave off tyranny in America, he argued. Truth, if not used "wantonly," must be reckoned by all reasonable men as a defense. Without the freedom of the press to utter the truth,

> "you must forever, remain ignorant of what your rulers do. ...
> "I never did think the truth as a crime,
> "for my soul has ever abhorred the thought that a free man
> "dared not speak the truth."

Hamilton was forty-nine when he died. He is buried in Trinity churchyard, a few blocks south of the World Trade Center site, so much a symbol of the financial new order that he, more than any other Founding Father, created.

INTRODUCTION TO

Hamilton's
Practice Manual[*]

P ractical Proceedings in the Supreme Court of the State of New York—By Alexr Hamilton. These words are penned on the first page of a small, foxed volume bound in boards with leather spine and corners belonging to the Association of the Bar of the City of New York. The manuscript totaling 177 pages is written on *Britannia* paper, a mark much used by the legal profession in the closing years of the colonial period and for some time thereafter. Following the manuscript itself are nine blank pages, also *Britannia* paper, of a slightly heavier weight. The first, second, and last sheets have a 1798 watermark. These pages are not numbered, and it seems probable that they were added to give bulk to the little book when it was put into its present binding. On the outside front cover are one

---

[*] NOTE: Reprinted with permission of Columbia University Press © 1964.
Editor: Julius Goebel, Jr.

identifiable and two unidentifiable signatures. On the outside back cover is written three times "Hamilton's Practice."

Practical Proceedings sets forth the procedure of the Supreme Court of New York and some of the substantive law of New York State. The evidence, shortly to be summarized, strongly indicates that this work was written by Hamilton at a time when New York's first constitution was but five years old and British troops still occupied New York City. It is the earliest known treatise on the practice of the independent State; yet it has received but passing mention or cursory description in the Hamilton biographies.[1] The treatise is published for the first time in the pages which follow. It furnishes a concise view of practice in New York when Hamilton came to the bar and is indispensable to an understanding of the procedure in many of the documents here published.

Hamilton's original manuscript has not been found, although diligent search has been made. Nevertheless, it is difficult not to be persuaded of the authenticity of the text here published. Since it is not in Hamilton's hand, it is probably one of the copies made by another student or a practitioner who was eager to gain for his own use a transcript of this only existing treatise on New York practice. The fact that on the inside of the front cover and on the flyleaf appears the signature of Abraham Van Vechten leads us to assume that the copy was his.[2] He was admitted to practice in 1783 and went on to become a well-known upstate lawyer, an ardent admirer of Hamilton and his associate in various cases. Whether or not he made

---

[1] See, for example, Miller, J. C., *Alexander Hamilton: Portrait in Paradox* (1959) (no mention of the treatise); 2 Hamilton, J. C., *History of the Republic Traced in the Writings of Alexander Hamilton* (1879) 282; 1 Mitchell, Alexander Hamilton (1957) 268. *But see* Mitchell, "Practical Proceedings in the Supreme Court of the State of New York," 11 *The Record of the Association of the Bar of the City of New York* (1956) 210-211.

[2] The signature on the cover is indisputably Van Vechten's as a comparison with his signatures preserved in the Van Vechten Manuscripts (NYSL) demonstrates. The flyleaf signature corresponds with an autograph preserved and interleaved in Gorham A. Worth, *Random Recollections of Albany from 1800 to 1808* ([Extra illus. ed., Albany J. Munsell 1866] vol. 2, p. 61 [NYSL]), and is a species of "copybook" signature.

the transcription is impossible to state, for the handwriting of the text itself does not resemble that of Van Vechten's copies of his earliest pleadings, although the discrepancy is not more marked than in the case of the script of rough and engrossed minutes done by the same court clerk.

Practical Proceedings very certainly came into the hands of Peter Gansevoort (1788-1876). He studied in the law offices of Bleecker and Sedgwick, and sometime prior to June, 1810, worked as a clerk in the Van Vechten and Van Schaick law offices at Albany.[3] The identifiable signature on the front cover is Gansevoort's. On the dorse of page 177 of the manuscript, the several attempts to render Van Vechten's signature are in a hand that resembles Gansevoort's florid script. It was by gift of Gansevoort's daughter Catherine Gansevoort Lansing (Mrs. Abraham Lansing) that our treatise came to the Association of the Bar.

Perhaps the most persuasive piece of external evidence pointing to Hamilton's authorship of the text of *Practical Proceedings* is a post-1800 revision of our text, written on paper watermarked 1802 and again in an unknown handwriting. This manuscript, recently acquired by Columbia University, is entitled *The Attorney's Practice in the Supreme Court of the State of New York*. Its authorship is also indicated by the words "By Alexr. Hamilton Esqe." hand-lettered at the top of the first page of the manuscript. Twenty of the original thirty-eight topics of *Practical Proceedings* are retained in the greatly modified *Attorney's Practice*. The text of these retentions is, with certain additions and deletions, substantially a paraphrase of the earlier text. The pages 23 and 24 missing from the manuscript of *Practical Proceedings* are supplied in our transcription from this later version.

It seems reasonable to surmise that *Attorney's Practice* is one of the last manuscript transcriptions made from the original or from a copy of Hamilton's treatise. The fact that the transcriber still attributed it to

---

[3] See letter, Peter Gansevoort to Anthony Van Schaick, Jun 5, 1811, Lansing-Gansevoort Papers (Ms. NYPL).

Hamilton and that so much of the two texts is similar is close to being decisive that Hamilton wrote *Practical Proceedings*. The internal references which place the date of transcription of *Attorney's Practice* between the years 1802 and 1803[4] indicate the esteem in which both Hamilton and his treatise were held. Contrary to a suggestion of one of Hamilton's biographers,[5] these dates in the *Attorney's Practice* show that *Practical Proceedings* continued to be of use to the profession or its students well after the publication of Wyche's *New York Supreme Court Practice* in 1794. *Attorney's Practice* contains not only a revision of over half of the subjects in *Practical Proceedings* but fifteen new subjects[6] and an eighty-two-page analysis of the second volume of Blackstone's *Commentaries*. While the changed title and the detail with which some of the passages of the earlier work are rearranged and organized in the later volume might be taken as some indication that Hamilton had a hand in the revision, nevertheless, the inclusion in *Attorney's Practice* of material from *Practical Proceedings* which contains error or conjecture argues against such a conclusion. Had Hamilton, as a seasoned practitioner, purposed to produce a thorough revision of *Practical Proceedings*, he surely would not have permitted to be carried forward in the new book some of his student estimates of what the law was, particularly when some of these were correctible from Wyche's printed volume.[7]

Wyche's book, the first published treatise, itself has some bearing on the matter of copies or revisions of *Practical Proceedings* because of

[4] Internal references to the date 1802 appear at 20 and 26 of *Attorney's Practice;* to the date 1803, at 79.

[5] 1 Mitchell, *Alexander Hamilton* (1957) at 581-582 n. 35.

[6] Most of these topics concern an analysis of new statutory material on such subjects as Detinue, Dower, Frauds, Tenures, Decents, Uses, Mortgage, and Account.

[7] Compare pages [34], [68], [69], and [74] in *Practical Proceedings* with pages 52, 54, 27-28, and 77, respectively, in *Attorney's Practice*. The last two conjectures, the first of which was incorrect, were easily verifiable in Wyche, William, *NY Supreme Court Practice* (1794) 29 and 106, respectively. All citations made to *Practical Proceedings* are to the original pagination in the manuscript. Original page numbers are indicated by brackets both here and within the manual as printed below.

a cryptic reference in the preface. Wyche speaks of having consulted "Some practical sketches in manuscript, one passing under the name of a personage of high respectability."[8] In the body of his text he closely paraphrases statements which appear in *Practical Proceedings*,[9] including an incorrect characterization of the New York writ of *capias* which appears on the first page of Hamilton's work.[10] If there was any "personage of high respectability" other than Hamilton who possessed manuscripts useful to a treatise writer, he remains unknown to us. Wyche's comment, therefore, and the transcription of an error not to say recurrent phrasing which is arrestingly similar to that in *Practical Proceedings* provide fair basis for the inference that the reference was to Hamilton and that the manuscript was *Practical Proceedings*.

There remains to be considered additional evidence regarding the authorship of *Practical Proceedings*. In the first place we have the testimony of Robert Troup that Hamilton wrote such a book while studying for the bar—testimony hardly to be impeached.[11] Troup was living with the Hamiltons and tutoring his friend when Hamilton was studying for the bar in 1782. Hamilton's son confirmed Troup's testi-

---

[8] Wyche, *NY Supreme Court Practice* (2d ed. 1794) ix.

[9] Compare Hamilton, *infra* p. [126] on "Reference": "The Matter afterwards proceeds as on an Inquiry, and when finished the Referrees make their Report & deliver it in Writing to the prevailing Party" with Wyche, *op. cit. supra* n. 8, at 243: "The matter is then considered in the same manner as on a writ of inquiry, and, when gone through, the referees make their report, and deliver it to the prevailing party." At page [137] *infra* Hamilton, writing on the topic "Bringing Money into Court," states: "if the Plaintiff accepts it as a full Satisfaction, then all further Proceedings to be staid, but if he does not accept it, then so much to be struck out of the Declaration; and if on Trial of the Issue more be found due to him than is tendered, that he shall Recover Costs if not, that then he shall pay Costs to the Defendant." Wyche's statement on the same subject, at page 106, reads: "if the plaintiff accept it as a full satisfaction, together with the costs thitherto incurred, then all further proceedings to be stayed; but if he does not accept it in full, then so much to be struck out of his declaration; and if, upon the trial more is found due to him than is paid in, he shall recover costs; if not, that he shall pay costs to the defendant."

[10] See *infra* n. 3, at p. 65, for a comparison of Wyche and Hamilton and an analysis of why the statement was in error.

[11] Schachner, "Alexander Hamilton Viewed by His Friends: The Narratives of Robert Troup and Hercules Mulligan," 4 *The William and Mary Quarterly* (1947) 215.

mony and asserted also that copies were made of Hamilton's text.[12] Secondly, the text itself supplies corroboration of the date of its original composition. For, barring two glosses and several obvious interpolations[13] which were made either at the time this copy was transcribed (probably between 1785 and 1787)[14] or at a later date by a subsequent owner, all internal references are to pre-1782 sources, the latest to a 1781 New York statute.[15]

Apart from the fact that Hamilton's little treatise is the first work in the field of private law by one of the great lawyers of the early Republic, it holds a place of some distinction in the legal history of New York. It serves, indeed, as a link between an older way of remembrancing the peculiarities of procedure in this jurisdiction and what was to come. We speak of peculiarities, for the basis both of practice and of substantive law in New York, as it was in other colonies, was the law of England. Each colony made its own accommodations, so that by 1776 the several jurisdictions differed in vari-

---

[12] 1 Hamilton, J. C., *Life of Hamilton* (1834) 398; 2 Hamilton, *loc. cit. supra* n. 1.

[13] The two glosses can be found at pages [28] and [127] *infra*. Probable interpolation is encountered at pages [17], [20], [26], and [110] *infra*.

[14] Transcribers of manuscript precedent books commonly used the current date for samples of legal documents they were copying as part of the text. Thus, in the precedent books mentioned *infra* n. 23, the Clinton manuscript has dates on sample writs running from 1786 to 1789, the Murray manuscript from 1731 to 1740, and the VanCortland manuscript from 1752 to 1760. The earlier dates always are toward the beginning of the volume and proceed through later dates to the end, with the exception of interpolations. Another exception to strict chronological order of the entire book derives from the practice of clerks and lawyers of establishing topic headings within their notebooks and entering sample documents under the appropriate heading as the authors encountered them in practice. In *Practical Proceedings* the dates of writs and bail pieces run from 1785 through 1787, indicating that the manuscript may have been three years in transcription. See *infra* pp. [17], [20], [26], [110]. That the date 1787 appears on pages [17] and [110] may indicate that the last part of the first section on Bail was not completed until that date.

The marginal addition to *Practical Proceedings* which appears at p. [38] of the transcript is in the same hand as the rest of the text and cites a statute enacted by the New York legislature on Feb 27, 1788. Note 42, p. 79, *infra*. The period from 1785 to 1788 corresponds to the three-year clerkship then required in New York, and it is a permissible inference that the transcriber of our copy of *Practical Proceedings* did his work during his clerkship, and when he had finished, brought it up to date at p. [38] by inserting the 1788 statutory modification.

[15] *Infra* p. [124].

ous particulars from each other as they did from their common source of reference. The latter is, to quote Coke out of context, "the golden metewand" by which one measures what is or is not a divergence. It is only necessary to compare *Practical Proceedings* with English law of the same period to discover the extent to which New York had departed from the paradigm.

In the light of what has already been remarked about the availability of English lawbooks in the Province of New York—the reports, abridgments, and a full range of texts—it may seem remarkable that the practice should have acquired native characteristics in some particulars at a fairly early date. Allowing even for a degree of judicial inexpertness in the early stages of development and for the fact that there were incidents for which the New Yorkers had no stomach, or which like outlawry would have been absurd to put to use, the chief reason for native idiosyncrasies was the fact that the Supreme Court of Judicature did not adhere to a single English model. It was not at all obligated to, for by the provincial Judicature Act of 1691[16] and the subsequent governors' ordinances of 1699 and 1704,[17] the powers of King's Bench, Common Pleas, and Exchequer were conferred upon it. Whether or not the intention was to leave to the bench the choice of forms from the variegated stock that these three English courts carried on their shelves, the fact is that there was selection and adaptation. There was some bending of forms to new uses and, as has been elsewhere shown in connection with the use of motions, some independent experimentation.[18]

Even in the eighteenth century certain developments in New York practice were of record in official minute books and files, although difficult to come upon. Many of the innovations were, to all appearances, not committed to writing when the bench made a ruling in a particular case. But having become a matter of general knowl-

---

[16] 1 *Col Laws NY* 229.

[17] See *infra* n. 1, at p. 63.

[18] Goebel and Naughton, *Law Enforcement in Colonial New York* (1944) 601-602.

edge among members of the bar, such would persist as usage.[19] The situation as respects procedure, therefore, came to resemble that of medieval times at the stage when the common law was preeminently a memory jurisprudence. There were, of course, no published reports of New York cases until the appearance of Coleman's slim volume in 1801. Not until 1804, when George Caines was appointed, was there an official reporter. We have Professor Eldon James's voucher that

> In the hundred years between the publication in 1687 of William Penn's gleanings from Lord Coke and the issuance of the American editions of Buller's Nisi Prius and Gilbert's Evidence in 1788, not a single book that could be called a treatise intended for the use of professional lawyers was published in the British Colonies and the American States.[20]

Since it was in the minds of New York judges and lawyers where reposed what Hamlet called the "quillets and quiddities" of practice, English books were of little avail to one not privy to this unwritten law. Indications of the state of affairs are furnished by *Practical Proceedings* in Hamilton's consistently anonymous references to the unrecorded rules of colonial or state practice as "our law" or similar expression.[21] On the other hand, his citation of English case law is often specific with reference to a reporter or a judge.[22] In New York's jurisprudence, the rule of decision endured in practice and memory while its genesis was forgotten.

---

[19] The casual remembrancing of such matter is illustrated by the manuscript entry on the index page of a copy of *New York Laws 1751* owned by the late Augustus Van Cortlandt: "Allowances agreed to by the Chief Justice for Travelling Charges to be taxed to the Lawyers on the Circuit and to be allowed in bills of costs." The per diem allowance for each cause was 13/4 and ranged from seventeen days to Albany to three days to Queens County. We have seen no other copy of this. Costs were fixed by Governor's ordinance, and it was consequently an unusual judicial intrusion into a forbidden field.

[20] James, "A List of Legal Treatises Printed in the British Colonies and the American States Before 1801," in *Harvard Legal Essays* (1934) 159.

[21] "The mode of Serving the Writ with us is . . . ." *infra* p. [3]; "It is the practice to . . . ." *infra* p. [4]; ". . . our Imparlance . . . ." *infra* p. [69]; "Note, With us we do not . . . ." *infra* p. [108]; ". . . probably it is so here . . . ." *infra* p. [132].

[22] See *infra* pp. [27], [32], [36], [41], [71], [80], [85], [175], citing Barnes, Salkeld, Wilson, Shower, Raymond, Carthew, Hardwick, Mansfield.

With respect to forms the situation was different. At a relatively early date it was common for lawyers to register and preserve them in so-called "precedent books"—a highly specialized type of common-place book of forms used in the various courts. These holograph volumes were not books of recorded decisions—as one might suppose from modern understanding of the word precedent—but were collections of writs, pleadings, judgment rolls, rules of court, tables of costs, and the like relating to particular causes of action.[23] In function they were similar to the files of procedural forms, pleadings, and "boiler plate" clauses which contemporary law firms maintain to avoid duplication of research. In colonial times, of course, and even later, these volumes served the additional purpose of preserving for

---

[23] Those that we have seen include works of DeWitt Clinton (c. 1787) (NYLI), William Livingston (c. 1760) (NYSL), Joseph Murray (c. 1735) (CULL), John Van Cortlandt (c. 1745) (NYHS), John Wickham (1766-1771) (a private, restricted manuscript which we were permitted to examine through the courtesy of Mr. David J. Mays of the Richmond Bar. This volume appears to have emanated from the office of Rudolph Ritzema, King's College 1758, who was a member of the lawyers' Moot.). Tentatively identified as the precedent book of Bartholomew Crannel, a resident of Dutchess County who deputized there for the provincial attorney general, is a volume in the Manuscript Division of the Library of Congress labeled "Common Place Book." It is a collection of forms of writs and rules of court dating from circa 1753 onward. At the end it contains material relating to Dutchess County entitled "Presedents respecting Special Bail of 1804." This book is the only one seen that contains directions regarding the tasks of an attorney after trial, which it lists under the title "Promtuary." For interest these tasks are here set forth:

"After every Court peruse your Dockett and note down

1t. What Writts are to be Issued.
2d What Declerations are to be filed or received.
3d What Pleas are to be filed or sent for from the adverse party.
4th In what Causes Bail is to be filed either by your Client or Adversary
5th What Letters are to be Written for Information from your Client or notice to be given, or for Bail Bonds.
6th What Causes are determined by agreement &c. in which Costs are to be drawn
7th What Judgments are to be made up, and Costs Taxed, and Executions to be Issued.
8th What Causes are brought to Issue, to be Tryed in a Succeeding Term, and take the proper steps for that purpose.
9th What Causes require Arguments to be prepared against the next Term.
10th Post. the Memorandums and Rules in your Dockett, and the Titles of the respective Causes, and then go thro' the Business contained in the above Articles and enter every step of your proceedings.
11th Prepare your Argument on points of Law.
12th Make out a Dockett for the succeeding Term."

reference what was unavailable in publications. The manuscript collections of William Livingston and DeWitt Clinton go beyond merely recording accepted forms of legal documents and contain brief statements of law on such procedural subjects as bail, process, execution, and the steps in bringing an action; that of John Wickham, the most extensive, contains a treatise of about two-thirds the length of *Practical Proceedings*. Most of those that have come to our attention are, however, form books and no more.[24] That these books were treasured is indicated by occasional specific bequests of such books or their inclusion in a general bequest of books and manuscripts.[25]

Practical Proceedings was an opus of a different genre from the traditional form books and for this reason was, as already remarked, a link between old ways of remembrancing and the new era of the printed practice books, of which Wyche's work was the first and Caines's *Summary of the Practice of the Supreme Court of New York* (1808) the second. The character of Hamilton's work was due to the circumstances under which it was composed, the result of the very unconventional way in which he prepared himself for the bar.

In colonial New York, as in eighteenth-century England, it was the rule for aspirants to the bar to pursue their studies in law offices,[26] where of course an apprentice's progress depended upon the

---

[24] Some useful details on procedure are also to be found in *Supreme Court Register A* of William Smith, Jr. (Ms. NYPL) and William Wickham, *Supreme Court Registers*, Libers A, B, and C (Ms. CULL).

[25] Thus, May Bickley, one-time Attorney General, bequeathed his papers and "all my manuscript presidents" to Will Sharpas. Wills, Liber 9, at 464 *sub* Jun 17, 1724 (Ms. NY County, Clerk of Surrogate). William Jamison bequeathed books and manuscripts to David Jamison. *Id.*, Liber 16 *sub* Apr 2, 1748. On the Murray bequest to King's College, see p. 5, *supra*. Lewis Morris, who died in 1762, left books he had purchased to his son Richard, and joint use of those he had from his father, as long as Richard continued in law practice. *Id.*, Liber 23, at 447. John Chambers (1764) divided his books and manuscripts between Augustus Van Cortlandt and John Jay. *Id.*, Liber 24, at 418. The manuscript Common Place Book of Chambers was donated to Columbia Law Library by Van Cortlandt's descendant.

[26] Discussion in Hamlin, *Legal Education in Colonial New York* (1939). Apprenticeship also prevailed in England. The Inns of Court had ceased to offer legal instruction in the last years of Charles II's reign, and remained merely a mechanism for being called to the bar. The myth has persisted that they were still places of instruction as they had once been. This illusion has

skill and interest of the practitioner who had undertaken to train him. We have some testimony from pre-Revolutionary law students about the rigors of training.[27] And for what retrospective value it may possess, we have a lament from one of Hamilton's first apprentices, Dirck Ten Broeck. He wrote to Simeon Baldwin in 1784 reminiscing about the joys of college life at Yale and then confided the following with regard to his apprenticeship with Hamilton:

> . . . but now instead of all the happiness once so near to view, I am deeply engaged in the Study of law, the attaining of which, requires the sacrafice of every pleasure, demands unremitted application: six long month's have passed since my commencing the study of this noble science, heavy for the most part have been the hours to me. . . .[28]

So far as the actual course of study on the eve of the Revolution was concerned, there survives that carefully laid out by William Smith Jr. which William Livingston also entered in his precedent book.[29] This course antedates the acceptance of Blackstone as a primer. It contains so much of what may be called "background study" that it may have been drawn with reference to a rule of the

---

strangely not been dissipated by the documented account in 6 Holdsworth, *History of English Law* (1924) 286-493 and 12 Holdsworth, *History of English Law* (1938) 15 *et seq*. The English barrister learned his law in a law office exactly as did his colonial brother.

[27] See the complaints of Peter van Schaak in Hamlin, *op. cit. supra* n. 26, at 43 and of William Livingston in *id.* at 167.

[28] Letter, Dirck Ten Broeck to Simeon Baldwin, Aug 15, 1784, Baldwin Family Papers (YUL). Hamilton remained a severe taskmaster, *vide* following directions for his son Phillip: "From the first of April to the first of October he is to rise not later than Six Oclock. The rest of the year not later than Seven. If Earlier he will deserve Commendation. Ten will be his hour of going to bed throughout the year. From the time he is dressed in the morning till Nine Oclock (the time for breakfast Excepted) he is to read law. At nine he goes to the office & continues there till dinner time. He will be occupied partly in the writing and partly in reading law. After Dinner he reads law at home till five O'clock. From this hour till seven he disposes of his time as he pleases. From Seven to ten he reads and studies whatever he pleases. From twelve on Saturday he is at liberty to amuse himself. On Sunday he will attend the morning Church. The rest of the day may be applied to innocent recreations. He must not Depart from any of these rules without my permission." Hamilton Papers (LC) (c. 1800).

[29] The curriculum published in Hamlin, *op. cit. supra* n. 26, at 197. It appears in Livingston, *Ms. Book of Precedents* at 139.

Supreme Court of 1767 that required a five-year clerkship and a certificate of qualification from an attorney of the court. The period of clerkship was curtailed to three years for those possessed of an A.B. degree.[30] The Smith-Livingston course required a great deal of book work. It made no mention of another phase of pedagogy—the copying of all manner of legal instruments that passed through a law office.[31] Presumably the educational merits of this lay in the ultimate transmission to the apprentice's intelligence of a command of form through the stultifying process of writing and rewriting. A conscientious preceptor would, one may hazard, be at pains to instruct on the content of forms and so, in the course of clerkship, the student might thus acquire some real understanding of procedural detail.

The Smith-Livingston curriculum concludes by quoting the "antient verses" which Sir Edward Coke commended to law students as a model "for the good spending of the day."[32] The time there allotted for various devotions exceeded that budgeted for law study, but the eighteenth century—that age of the Enlightenment—had obviously rectified this. In any event Hamilton's period of study for the bar was so brief and so concentrated that there was small time for orisons. The Supreme Court in 1778 had cut down the time of clerkship to three years.[33] It said nothing about a qualifying certificate, but it provided for a bar examination. In January, 1782, the court further relaxed standards by suspending the clerkship rule in favor of war veterans who had directed their prewar studies to the profession of the law.[34] This suspension was good only through the April term.

[30] Ms. Mins NY Sup Ct Judicature 1766-1769, 180 sub May 1, 1767 (HR).

[31] Warren, History of the American Bar (1913) 166.

[32] Coke, Littleton, 64b.

[33] Ms. Mins NY Sup Ct Judicature 1775-1781, 177 (HR). This is embodied in a special rule Apr 23, 1779, providing for examination and admission of attorneys of the inferior Courts of Common Pleas. The rule was made because of the absence of former Supreme Court practitioners due to the disturbed times.

[34] Ms. Mins NY Sup Ct Judicature 1781-1783, 92-93 (HR).

When Hamilton left the Continental Army from Washington's camp at Yorktown, Virginia, late in October, 1781,[35] the three-year clerkship was still the rule. When he reached Albany he contracted an illness that had him "in and out of bed" past the end of December.[36] It was thus improbable that he could have entered fully upon his legal training until January, the month the rule was changed. Nevertheless, by the following July he was admitted an attorney qualified to practice before the Supreme Court.[37] In October, 1782, followed his admission as counsel,[38] the New York equivalent of the English barrister; and some time prior to October, 1783, he had qualified both as solicitor and counsel in Chancery.[39]

That Hamilton was able in a span of six months to achieve a sufficient mastery of the law to satisfy the examining judges may be laid to the fact that he came to his technical studies conversant with works then regarded as necessary groundwork to such studies. As already noted, he had been reading around in the law while yet a student at King's College.[40] This was on his own initiative, for there was nothing then in the college curriculum to have opened the door to the literature of the law.[41] But Hamilton's polemical pamphlets disclose that he had been exposed to works on the law of nations and nature then deemed a prerequisite to the study of English law itself—Burlamaqui, Grotius, Locke, Montesquieu, and Pufendorf. Beyond this he had

[35] 1 Mitchell, *op. cit. supra* n. 5, at 578 n. 59.

[36] 2 *PAH* 684.

[37] 3 *PAH* 122.

[38] 3 *PAH* 189.

[39] Solicitor and counsel in Chancery were analogous to the status of attorney and counsel in the Supreme Court. No document is available to establish the exact date on which Hamilton qualified as solicitor and counsel in the Court of Chancery, but an oath for faithful execution of office which Hamilton took on October 20, 1783, recites that he then had those qualifications. 3 *PAH* 471. Hamilton was admitted to practice before the United States Supreme Court on February 22, 1796. *Mins US Sup Ct, sub* Feb 22, 1796 (Ms. Natl Archs).

[40] *Supra* p. 5.

[41] On the alleged professorship of law at King's College and the absence of proof that lectures even on natural law were given, see *History of the School of Law, Columbia University* (Goebel ed. 1955) 8-9.

read in Blackstone, Coke's *Reports*, Beawes's *Lex Mercatoria,* and obviously some work on principles of feudal tenures.[42] He resorted to the texts of both English statutes and acts of Assembly in a way to disclose an aptitude for dealing with such technical matter.

These early studies were important in an immediately practical way, for when Hamilton appeared at the April, 1782, term—the time that the suspension of the three-year clerkship was due to end—he could declare, as he did, that his studies had been directed to the profession of law. He then prayed for an extension of time as he was as yet unprepared for an examination. This was granted.[43]

In addition to assistance with his studies by his friend Troup, Hamilton had the boon of access to James Duane's library,[44] then also being used by John Lansing Jr., future Chief Justice of the New York Supreme Court and later Chancellor of the State.[45] Judging from the citations in some of Duane's briefs—not, of course, an infallible test—this must have been a very good library, preeminently the best then located in the little city of Albany, a place not distinguished for its bar in colonial times.

Recourse to Duane's books could both broaden and deepen a student's understanding of the law. But as already indicated, books alone could not supply the sort of technical command of New York practice of which a postulant for admission would stand in need. This was, of course, the point where a preceptor experienced in the "practick part" of the law was close to being indispensable. How helpful Troup could have been is problematical. He was himself preparing for his examination, and although he had studied before the war first with Thomas Smith of Haverstraw and then with John Jay, he had finished his training with a New Jersey lawyer, William Paterson,

---

[42] Hamilton, *The Farmer Refuted* (1775), in 1 *PAH* 81-144; Hamilton, *The Quebec Bill: Part One* (1775), in 1 *PAH* 165-168; 1 Mitchell, *op. cit. supra* n. 5, at 59.

[43] 3 *PAH* 82.

[44] 3 *PAH* 88.

[45] *DAB sub nom.* Lansing.

later Justice of the United States Supreme Court.[46] New Jersey practice was cut on much the same pattern as that of New York, but the mere fact that New York lawyers entered New Jersey forms in their precedent books indicates an awareness of differences.[47] With Troup's most recent training in "foreign law," as Thomas Jefferson ticketed the laws of Virginia's sister states,[48] there is reason to doubt how well initiated he may have been in the nuances of New York practice. However, he was admitted in April, 1782,[49] and he was thus in a position to advise Hamilton on the nature of questions put in the course of the examination.

All this may well have some bearing on how Hamilton put together his manual. Hamilton was spared the drudgery of copying legal instruments that a long clerkship entailed, but he was deprived of sustained counsel on their use and significance. In 1782 this was a particular handicap, for although litigation in the Supreme Court was conducted substantially as it had been before the war, under the mandate of Article 35 of the State Constitution the question of what Acts of Parliament and what portions of the common law were in force on April 15, 1775—and thus to be deemed received into the law of New York State—was a question only this court could settle. On the difficulties entailed, we have the testimony of James Kent from the year 1786.[50]

---

[46] *DAB sub nom.* Troup.

[47] E.g., the manuscript *Murray Precedent Book,* 18, 61, 105 (CULL) or the *Ms. Livingston Precedent Book,* 40, 51, 118 (NYSL).

[48] 2 Sowerby, *Catalogue of the Library of Thomas Jefferson* (1953) 384.

[49] *DAB sub nom.* Troup; A Roll of the Attornies of the Supreme Court of the State of New York (Ms. HR).

[50] ". . . We must enter likewise at least in this State into the whole Detail of the English Institutions, & study with as much Curiosity & attention as tho we were preparing for the Courts at Westminster the whole complicated Fabrics as well as the particular Branches of their celebrated System of Laws—For the whole Body of the English Statute & Common Law that is not directly incompatible with the Independency of our Government applies of Course to this State & is equally binding as our own Statutes—This is to be understood only of those Laws that are not controuled by some subsequent Regulation of our own & that were in force in England down to their Revolution in 1688. For since that time their *Statutes* did not apply

Thus, by circumstances, Hamilton's manual was a thing of his own making. It bears all the earmarks of student work, not that of a practitioner seasoned in New York law. Indeed, the cursory fashion in which Hamilton deals with some of the thirty-eight topics into which the work is divided bears a striking resemblance to the sort of synthesis which a law student might devise today if interested in procedural aspects of law for a particular examination.[51] Furthermore, the lack of any orderly sequence in the arrangement of the topics suggests that the writing on a particular subject was done after reading some book and searching out cases or statutes, and the heading next following might well derive from a second source. Very obviously whatever the main source for "Process" and "Bail," it did not deal with "Ac Etiam" or, if it did, Hamilton was hardly aware of the fact that the three subjects needed to be considered together. Whether or not Hamilton realized this as his studies progressed, he later inserted a section on *Ac Etiam*.[52] There are other features that bear out our hypothesis, in particular the strange placement of Judgment and Execution, which one would expect to conclude a practice manual. The manual ends instead with Trespass in Ejectment as a species of supplement.

It will be noticed that in places where Hamilton did not comprehend the product of his research he freely admitted it, in one place

unless we were *expressly named* (as we had a Legislature of our own) & *then they did*—Tho I think that Admission was an unwarrantable & supreme exertion of sovereignty, subversive in Effect of our independent Rights & directly contrary to the Fundamental Principle upon which we begun the new Revolution—So that you see the English Common Law is part of the Law of this State & can only be discovered & known by searching into the Decisions of the English Courts which are the only Evidence of the Common Law & these Decisions are regarded with us as *authentic Evidence* of the Common Law & therefore are cited as *Precedents binding* with us even down to the year 1776. . . . I believe there never was a Commonwealth before this of New York under the Sun whose Municipal Laws required an Examination so various so extensive & so profound, & which involved in them so much splendid & useful as well as so much tedious & antiquated Learning." Letter, James Kent to Simeon Baldwin, Jul 18, 1786, Baldwin Family Papers (YUL).

[51] See *infra* p. [175]: "Question tho' simple, is generally made one of the bugbear Questions on an Examination."

[52] *Attorney's Practice* combines "Ac Etiam" with "Bail."

saying "Indeed I do not understand the rule"[53] and in another, "this proceeding seems to be without use, nor do the Books explain its Intention, but it seems it is still followed."[54] More than once Hamilton states as a conjecture a proposition which an attorney with very little practical experience would have known. Thus, with regard to the form of the motion by which an attorney might compel the clerk at *nisi prius* to return the *postea,* Hamilton states, "I suppose the Rule is, That the Clerk of *nisi prius* return the Postea, or shew cause why an Attachment should not Issue against him."[55] While explaining the operation of statutory reference and the manner in which motion may be made to enforce a master's conclusions, Hamilton states, "I take it for Granted he gives the usual Notice of his Intended motion to the opposite Party and a Copy of the Report."[56] Again, lacking practical knowledge of the form of a rule of court, this time relating to tender, Hamilton begins his conjectured characterization of the rule "I imagine ordering" and finishes the sentence "not having seen the Rule this is only conjecture."[57]

Whether or not Hamilton was fully aware of the fact, in his efforts to inform himself he employed what may be described as a comparative legal study. As already remarked, he cited specific English sources and often alluded to anonymous colonial or state law. Our footnotes not only indicate the authorities referred to by Hamilton but also enlarge upon some of the areas wherein New York law diverged from English rules. Using English law as a basis for evaluation, instances of both sophistication and naïvete can be found in the state law. For example, speaking of jury process, Hamilton notes that New York's procedure differs from that of England and then continues, "some say it [the English writ of *distringas*] is still proper to be

[53] See *infra* p. [150].
[54] See *infra* p. [101].
[55] See *infra* p. [17].
[56] See *infra* p. [126].
[57] See *infra* p. [137].

used where there is a Jury of View, *but there seems to be no Reason for this.*[58] Analysis of why New York law and English law should differ on this subject reveals that colonial lawyers apparently were aware of the implications of a change which had occurred in English law and took advantage of it by simplifying (and therefore improving) their own jury process whereas England continued a fourteenth-century procedure which for nearly fifty years had been unnecessary.[59] The phrase in Hamilton's statement we have emphasized indicates his awareness of the somewhat involved reason for this sophistication. Such understanding of how English procedure as adapted was applied in New York stands in sharp contrast to the manner in which the first process of the state operated. Annotations to the pages of *Practical Proceedings* dealing with process show that confusion over the identical procedural purpose of the King's Bench Bill of Middlesex and the Common Pleas writ of *capias* was egregious,[60] and although adequate explanation of the writs was accessible in Blackstone's *Commentaries*[61] and Bohun's *Institutio Legalis,*[62] it appears that even after the lapse of a century, New York lawyers had no more idea why they were using two different instruments to do the same task than they had understanding of the history and function of these processes in England.

Some feeling for Hamilton's temperament can be gained from the tone in which *Practical Proceedings* is written. The resignation and the dry humor with which he approached his studies are revealed by such statements as "the Court . . . lately acquired . . . some faint Idea that the end of Suits at Law is to Investigate the Merits of the Cause, and not to entangle in the Nets of technical Terms."[63] He regarded

[58] See *infra* p. [10]. (Emphasis added.)
[59] See *infra* n. 6, at p. 67.
[60] See *infra* nn. 1 & 2, at pp. 63 & 64.
[61] 3 Blackstone, *Commentaries* (1771) 281-288.
[62] Bohun, *Institutio Legalis: An Introduction to the Laws of England* (3d ed. 1724) 18-21, 181-184.
[63] See *infra* p. [42].

inconsistent pleading to be "among the Absurdities with which the Law abounds"[64] and, speaking of the rationale by which lawyers of his time determined which actions could be joined in the same declaration, he comments, "There is the usual Confusion in this Doctrine."[65] Hamilton spoke for generations of law students past and present when he recognized with appropriate disdain that the action of trespass in ejectment "is a Creature of Westminster Hall & subsists Chiefly upon Fiction."[66]

Where Hamilton had difficulty in formulating a rule of law, or where he conjectured about what the law was or should have been, effort has been made in the editing to find the reason for the difficulty and to determine whether or not his guesses were correct. Although this endeavor uncovered several mistakes[67] and, indeed, although the treatise is in error on other points which were not stated as conjecture,[68] criticism of Hamilton is hardly warranted, for time was at his heels; and, as already remarked, procedural law of that time had its uncertainties and even the most recent English lawbooks were of limited value in determining this law for the state. Some of the statements in *Practical Proceedings* which today can be judged to have been incorrect may well have expressed the views of the contemporary bench and bar, and in that sense were then good law.[69]

Just as Hamilton encountered difficulty in ascertaining points of substantive law and procedure which were not set forth clearly in lawbooks available to him, or whose sources he could not consult because they were unwritten products of the New York colonial and state judiciary, so we have had difficulties in determining the accura-

---

[64] See *infra* pp. [49-50].

[65] See *infra* p. [119].

[66] See *infra* p. [161].

[67] See *infra* Practical Proceedings, nn. 71, 94, 142.

[68] See *infra* Practical Proceedings, nn. 3, 87, 122, 128, 148.

[69] This is particularly true with regard to Hamilton's views of reception of English law. See the statement of Jones and Varick, *infra* n. 128, at p. 115.

cy of statements made by Hamilton. Treatises on New York law written after Hamilton's time can be used only with great caution because
Practical Proceedings was written when the law was in an unusual state
of flux that abated somewhat only after the great statutory revision
undertaken in 1786 was finished. While those reports and treatises to
which Hamilton adverted by citation or reference (and which are set
forth in the book list as among the volumes almost certainly available
to him during his period of study) were used as a point of departure
for our research, completeness required resort to interpolation
between preceding English or New York Colonial law and subsequent
English and New York State law. Because much of the practice and
many of the terms described or employed in Hamilton's text are foreign to both layman and lawyer today, annotation digresses more
than occasionally in order to orient the reader so that he may better
appreciate the subject of text or footnote. To permit such explana-
tions to be read with facility "Editor's Notes" have been employed in
some instances in this chapter wherein authorities supporting
explanatory notes have been separated from the notes themselves.
Readers desiring to analyze substantive law will find assistance in the
exhibits of procedural documents which are printed beginning at
page 107, immediately following Hamilton's text.

Practical Proceedings in the Supreme Court of the State of New York. — By Alex Hamilton

PROCESS

*J*f the Person against whom you intend to bring your action lives in the County in which the Supreme Court usually sits the first Process is a Bill of that County at present a Bill of Albany in Imitation of the Bill of Middlesex—[1]

If the Person resides in a different County your first Process must be a Capias[2] which is a Writ compounde[d] of the Capias of Common Pleas and the Bill of Midd[le]sax of the Kings Bench—[3]

If the Person is not found in the County in which your first Writ issues in the first Case you must sue out a Latitat[4] in the second a Testatum Capias—[5]

---

[1] See n. 1, p. 63. See Exhibits A-1 and A-2.

[2] See n. 2, p. 64.

[3] See n. 3, p. 65. See Exhibits B-1, B-2, and B-3.

[4] See Exhibit C. The forms of the latitat used in New York Province and in colonial New Jersey were apparently identical. See Livingston, William, *Ms. Precedent Book* (c. 1760) 33, where the jurisdiction is cited as New Jersey.

[5] See n. 4, p. 67.

If the Person is not found on the first Writ and you expect afterwards to take him in the same [2] County in which the first Issued you sue out an Alias Bill of Albany, or Capias and a pluries of the same; and if it be still necessary to repeat the Customary Practice is to begin a new.* After a Pluries; the Alias differs from the first only by inserting the words "as it was before commanded you" or, "as we before commanded you," and ~~that~~ the Pluries by Inserting these words "as it hath more then once been[7] commanded you," or, "as we have more the[n] onece commanded you."

When you have Occasion for either of these Writs you must make it out in the established Form, and a praecipe to be left at the Office get it sealed by the Clerk of the Court and give it to the Sheriff to be executed—Note there must a Praecipe for the Office with every Writ According to the Natu[re] of it either may be Tested one Day and returned the next—

If the Sheriff takes the Person if the Action requires only common Bail, the Defendant must Indorse his Appearance on the Back [3] of the Writ to this Effect, "I promise to appear at the Return of the within Writ and pray the Court to enter my appearance accordingly" A.B. "if the Action requires special Bail the Defendant with two Sureties enters into a Bail Bond to the Sheriff, which usually in [sic] double the sum specified in the Writ, sometimes an Attorney will engage in the first Instance to appear for the Defendant, and he Indorses for the Defendant thus, "I Promise an engage, to appear in Behalf of the within named A-B. at the Return of the within Writ and pray the Court to enter my Appearance accordingly (C-D. Atty)."—

If the Sheriff cannot find the Defendant he must return a *non est inventus*, "the within named A-B. is not found in my Bailwic (E.F.-Sheriff)."—

The mode of Serving the Writ with us is by the Sheriff touching the Body of the Person, & informing him that he has such a Writ - against him, explaining to him the Contents and if required shewing to him the Writ, but if he flies the Sheriff may proclaim his Business aloud and it will be deemed sufficient the Sheriff is Obliged to [4] take good Bail, or he is liable to an Action, but if the Defendant will not promise Appearance in case of

---

* This is disputed, and the way seems to be to sue out a Pluries after pluries till Deft. be taken.—[6]

[6] See n. 5, p. 67.

[7] The word *been* is inserted with a caret in different handwriting.

Practical Proceedings in the
Supreme Court of the State of
New York. — Say Alex Hamilton

By ALex Hamiltr.

Process.

If the Person against whom you intend to bring
your action lives in the County in which the Supreme Court usually sits the first Process is a Bill
of that County at present a Bill of Albany in Imitation of the Bill of Middlesex —

If the Person resides in a different County your first
Process must be a Capias which is a Writ companied
of the Capias of Common Pleas and the Bill of Middlesex of the Kings Bench —

If the Person is not found in the County in which
your first Writ issues in the first case you must sue
out a Latitat in the second a Testatum Capias

If the Person is not found on the first Testatum
you expect afterwards to take him in the

First Page of *Practical Proceedings*
Courtesy Association of the Bar of the City of New York

Common Bail or put in Bail to the Sheriff, where the Writ requires it the Sheriff must take him to Goal.—

It is the practice to teste the Writs on the last Day of the preceeding Term and make them returnable the ~~Day in Bank, or the~~ first Day in the Subsequent Term; the Writs of the Court may be Tested before the Cause of Action arose, but must be executed Afterwards but Originals are abateable if tested before the Cause of Action arose.—

The next Stap when the Writs are Returned & the Defendant engages to appear is for the Plts. Attorney to move the Court for a Rule that the Sheriff bring in the Body—*sedente Curia* or be amerced 40/—and that Defendant plead in 20 Days after Declaration or Judgment; it is not usual actually to move for this Rule, as it is a Rule of course but you must enter it on your Dagget, and the Clerk of the Court will Copy it in his Minutes; with us the Defendant must take Notice of this Rule of Court, tho', in [5] England the Plaintiff serves it upon him—N[B] all our Rules are 20 Days Rules Except in a few Cases.—

If the Defendant is in Custody the Rule must be that he plead in 20 Days after Declaration is served on the Sheriff or Person in whose Custody he i[s] or Judgment; the Defendant on this Rule ha[s] 20 Days after the End of the Term exclusively to file common Bail or put in Bail to the Action as the Case may Require, and he must give immediate Notice in Writing to the Plaintiffs Attorney, but the Notice in the last Case mu[st] specify the Places of residence of the Bail, the[ ] Additions &ca. The Plaintiff has 20 Days after Notice to make his Exceptions to the Bail, & if none are made in that Time, they become absolute; the present practice is to file common Bail at once with the Clerk of the Court. The Plaintiff has by the Course of the Court, two Ter[ms] to Declare in including the one in which th[e] Writ is returnable; but he may immediat[ely] After Notice of Bail being filed deliver Declaration the Manner of putting in Bail is to make out a Bail Piece on a Piece of Parchme[nt] and in case of Common Bail filing the [Bail] Piece with the Cl[erk of] the Court a[ ][6] before. In Case of special Bail the Defendant with his two Sureties before one of the Judges of the Court, or in a Country Cause before one of the Commissioners authorized for that Purpose & enters into a Recognizance. If the Defendant does not file common Bail the Plaintiff must do it for him with these words indorsed on the Bail Piece "filed according to the Statute."—**8**

The Recognizance of the Bail put in the County must be sent to one of the Judges of the Court within 20 Days, allowed by the Rule, and Notice must be given within the same Time.—When the Defendant or his Atty is to be found, the Plaintiffs Attorney must serve him with a Copy of the Declaration; When he is not to be found the Declaration must only be filed in the Clerks Office.—

Note regularly, a Copy of the Declaration shou[ld] in all Cases be left at the Clerks Office.—

After Declaration served the Defendant has 20 Days to plead within which time he mu[st] deliver his plea to the Plaintiffs Attorney and filing a Copy of it, or the Plaintiff may sign an Interlocutory [Jud]gment, or if the Actio[n] [7] be in Debt a final Judgment which is done upon the Back of the Declaration in the Office thus, "I enter Judgment in this Cause for want of a Pl[ea] A.B. Atty."—but this esteemed captious practice and seldom used, it is usual for the Plaintiff to wait till the next Term, and if no Plea is delivered in the meantime, to move the Court for Judgment for want of a Plea, which is done thus, "The Defendant in this Cause having neglected according to the Rule I pray Judgment *nisi causa,*" you ought regularly to serve a Copy of the Rule.—

If the Plaintiff does not declare before the End of the Second Term the Defendant may lay him under a Rule to declare in 20 Days or be non pross'd; which Rule he must Serve upon him and if he does not declare before the Rule expires the Defendant may move next Court for a non pros.

If the Defendant pleads in Time & Issue is joined the Plaintiff must bring on the Trial in the first triable Term Subsequent to that in whi[ch] Issue is Joined, otherwise the Term after the Defendant may move the Court for a non pr[os] for want of his having brought the Cause on [ ] Trial in the Course of the Courts; this Mot[ion] [8] regularly and according to the Books ought to be founded on Affidavit but it is said this is not the Custom with us.—

---

8 An Act to prevent frivolous and vexatious Arrests, 12 Geo 1, c. 29, sec. 1 (1725).

In all these Cases ~~two~~ four Days Notice exclusive must be given of the intended Motion to the opposite Party and regularly an Affidavit of the Service of that Notice ought be produced when the Motion is made, also it is a general Rule in special Motions founded on Affidavit to Accompany the Notice of your intended Motion with a Copy of your Affidavit.—

If the Defendant rather then nonpross the Plaintiff chooses to bring the Matter to Trial he may sue out a Ven[ire][9] Provisoe Clause in it, "Provided that if two Writs thereupon come to You, you shall execute only one of them," but this is now intirely disused, as the Plaintiff by not appearing at the Trial may bring the Matter to the same Point of a Nonpross; He must previously apply to the Court for Leave to bring on the Cause by Provisoe.—

When the Defendant proceeds by Provisoe, he must give the Notice of Trial &c: instead of [9] the Plaintiff—Whether you proceed by Provi[so] or nonpross, if the Plaintiff has not entered h[is] Issue with the Clerk of the Court you must [   ] him under a Rule to do it in 20 Days—Notic[e] of Trial must be given when the Defendan[t] lives within 40 Miles of the Place of Trial for eight Days beforehand; when beyond 40 Miles 14 Days these are computed Miles—Notice must be given to a Judge at the sam[e] Time. If the Plaintiff finds Afterwards that he cannot conveniently bring on the Trial at the Time appointed he must cou[nter]mand the Notice, in the first Case ~~2~~ 4 Days before the Trial, in the last 6, if he does not, the Defendant on Affidavit of Attendan[ce] and necessary Expences, will recover Costs; he must move the Court for them and give the usual Notice of a Special Motion to the Plaintiff who may controvert it if he can.

When the Cause is Notified for Trial the Pa[r]ties must Subpoena their Witnesses, by deliver[ing] to each a Subpoena Ticket with a Shilling & shewing him the Subpoena itself.—

The Plaintiff must sue out a Ven[ire] for summoning the Jury tested the last Day of the preceeding Term & returnable the first [10] of the next Term as is usual in general, and Deliver to the Sheriff; there must be in each

---

9 In this section of the manuscript *venire* often appears as venue. So as not to confuse the reader, *venue* is interpolated as *ven[ire]*. Hamilton's frequent failure to dot the letter "i" could have been easily misinterpreted by a transcriber not well versed in the law. The scribe of *Attorney's Practice* may have been better informed. See Exhibit D for writ of venire.

Ven[ire] this Clause Directed by an Act of our Legislature[10] "each of whom has a Freehold in Lands Tenements" & Rents in his own Right or in the Right of his Wife, of the Value of sixty pounds" if in the Mayors Court you add "or personal Estate of the same Value." When the Trial is to be in the Country there must be a nisi prius Clause in Ven[ire].—

Note we do not make use of the *Distringes*[11] or *Habeas corpus*,[12] as in England tho the Form is still preserved in making out the Records;[13] some say it is still proper to be used where there is a Jury of View, but there seems to be no Reason for this, nor is it always practised. In case after a Jury has been summoned in a Cause and the Ven[ire] returned and the Trial postponed you may use a *Distringes* to bring it on again.—

The Jurors must be summoned six Days exclusive before the Day of Trial, and either Party is intitled to a Copy of the Panel from the Sheriff five Days before the Return of the Ven[ire]

[11] When you wish to have a Jury of View you must proceed thus; The Party who wishes it makes Affidavit that he is acquainted with the Premises in Dispute and that he is informed and verily belives a previous View will be necessary; upon this Affidavit he moves the Court, having given two Days Notice of his Motion, for a Rule for such a Jury, which will be made ordering the Sheriff on a certain Day, (some convenient Day before hand) to return into the Clerks Office a Panel of 48 Freeholders or as many as the Court shall think proper, and out of these Parties shall by consent or Ballot take six or more to have a View of the Premises some Day before the Trial, which will be shewn to them by shewers appointed by the Court. When this Rule is Obtained the Party applying for it must send it to the Sheriff who will return the Panel accordingly, when h[e] has done it the Party must take it out of the Office and give Notice to the Opposite [12] Party Clerks[14] office to attend at a Judges Chamber[14] for the purpose of Striking the Clerk

---

[10] An Act for the Returning of Able and Sufficient Jurors, and for the better Regulation of Juries, 3 *Col Laws NY* (1741) 185 (continued and made perpetual in 1746 by 3 *Col Laws NY* 599).

[11] See Exhibit E.

[12] *Habeas corpora juratorum.*

[13] See n. 6, p. 67. See Exhibit F.

[14] The words *a Judges Chamber* and *Judge*, as well as the marginal notations *Clerks office* and *Clerk*, are underscored and overscored in the original manuscript, apparently indicating a reader's ques-

Jury; the Parties attend and strick the Jury accordinly, affter which a list of their Names is made and the Judge[14] certifies at the Bottom "The above are a Jury to have a View of the Premises in Dispute between AB & CD—This list with Panel annexed to Ven[ire] are sent to the Sheriff who must warn the Persons and accompany them to the place of View. When he makes out his Panel of Jurors for the Trial of the Cause he must place these at the Head of the List, who will be first sworn and cannot* be challenged—It is Customary to Strike 12 that at least 6 may attend I am not certain in this Case whether the Array can be challenged.—

Note the Array can be challenged.—

In a Cause of Great Importance one of the Parties may wish for a special Jury, and then he must move the Court for a Rule, having given Notice as before, tho this is not necessary by the Books of Practice Attorneys Guide 139.[15] The Court will make a Rule Directing the Sheriff to return his Book of Freeholders into the Clerks Office and the Parties with the Clerk to attend at the Judges Chamber where the Clerk shall in-[13] differently take from the Book of Freeholders 48 Persons, from which each Party shall at his Pleasure strike out 12 and the Remaining 24 shall be a Jury for the Trial of the Cau[se] the Party applying for the Rule, serves the Rule upon the Sheriff, and when he has returned his Book of Freeholders, having previously concerted a Day with the Judge gives Notice to the Clerk and opposite Party to Attend at the Judges Chamber and proceed to strick the Jury.—When the Jury is Struck a list certifyed by the Judge as in the Former Case,[16] is sent with the Venire to

---

tion about the accurateness of the description of selecting a jury of view. A "Quere" in the margin at p. 10 of *Attorney's Practice* shows that this point also troubled a reader of that book. Nevertheless, according to *NY Laws,* 9 Sess 1786, c. 41, sec. 18, the procedure described in *Practical Proceedings* and in *Attorney's Practice* is correct. *But see* n. 16, *infra.*

This statute, entitled "An Act for regulating Trials of Issues and for returning able and sufficient Jurors," is the act referred to in the manuscript footnote at the end of this paragraph. It was reenacted in *NY Laws,* 24 Sess 1801, c. 98, sec. 21. This notation appears to be in the same hand as the rest of the transcription. See also n. 42, *infra.*

* by an Act passed in 1786 they may be challenged

[15] *The Attorney's Compleat Guide in the Court of the King's Bench, by an attorney of the court* (London 1773) 139.

[16] Hamilton probably was incorrect in stating that the list is "certifyed by the Judge as in the Former Case." By *NY Laws,* 9 Sess 1786, c. 41, sec. 19, and unlike the procedure for the jury of view, the parties struck the jury in the presence of the clerk and the list so obtained was certified by the clerk. This statute was reenacted in *NY Laws,* 24 Sess 1801, c. 98, sec. 22. *Attorney's Practice,* at p. 11, reflects this procedure.

the Sheriff, the extra Expence is at all Events paid by the Party applying and other extra Expences must also be paid by him unless the Judge before whom the Trial is had will certify that the Cause Required a special Jury; this Jury is liable to Challenges like any other.—

Regularly before Causes are brought on for Trial they are entered with the Clerk of the Court, and brought on in the order in which they are entered; if they are not Tried according to the Notification, they stand over as *Remanets* and take their Turn as Junior Caus[es] [14] the Defendant is bound to Attend until the Court rises. Should the Defendant find it necessary to put off the Cause for want of Witnesses he must move the Court on Affidavit setting forth that the Witness is a Material Witness in the Cause without whom it would be unsafe for him, to proceed to Trial, that he has been Subpoened[17] and his necessary expences tendered him, but that he has not Attended (or that he has taken out a Subpoena for him and has endeavoured but had not been able to serve it) he may set forth what has prevented him, but this seems not necessary; should the Witness have gone beyond Sea or out of the State he must set that forth, and the Time he is Expected to return The Court will commonly put off the Trial, but it remains at their Discretion.—

When the Trial is over & the Jury have given their Verdict, it is incumbent on the Atty for Plaintiff to move for a Judgment if the Verdict be in his Favor *nisi Causa*, the Rule need not be served but Notice must be taken of it of Course and the opposite Party has four Days to apply for a New Trial or move in Arrest of Judgment.—

[15] The Application for a New Trial must be fou[n]ded on something extrinsic of the Record, as—Misbehaviour in the Jury Misdirection of th[e] Judge, Refusal of admitting proper Evidence Surprize or excessive Damages.—

The Arrest of Judgment must be founded on something intrinsic to the Record, as want of Substance or Form in the Declaration, Pleadings &c— whatever may be a foundation for [ ] Arrest of Judgment would have been good on Demurrer but not *vice versa*, for there are many things that are cured

---

The marginal notations and manuscript markings at p. [12] (see n. 14, *supra*) which seem to question the location for the striking of a jury and the certification of the list should have been directed not to the jury of view but to the struck jury.

[17] See Exhibit G.

by the Statute of Jeofail[18] after Verdict, which would have been fatal before—
In general whatever Defen[se] may be Supposed to have been supplyed [by]
Evidence is Cured by the Verdict—It is a general Rule that though After
Motion for a new Trial you may move in Arrest of Judgment, yet you cannot
afte[r] Motion for an Arrest of Judgment mov[e] for a new Trial; but in Cases
of gross Misbehaviour in the Jury the Rule has been Departed from—

[16] Also after the Rule *nisi causa* is out the Plaintiff may immediately
sign Judgment yet the Defendant may move in Arrest of Judgment before the
Judgment is actually signed; when it is said there are four Days to move for a
new Trial or in Arrest of Judgment this is on a Supposition that there are so
many Days Remaining in the Term after the Motion; if there are not you
must content yourself with less, but then the Plaintiff cannot take out
Execution till the four Days are expired; but if the Motion is made on the very
last Day of the Term you have first four Days of the next Term—

In Country Causes the Clerk of Nisi prius ought to Return the Posteas
on the first Day in the Bank, regularly he ought to be laid under a Rule for
this purpose, but as he saldom omits it, it is not done; sometimes the Party in
whose Favor the Verdict has been given, if he sees the Clerk in Court will tell
him that if he does not Return the Posteas, he will be Obliged to lay him
under a Rule & if he shou[ld] [17] not return them it must be done. I suppose th[e] Rule is, That the Clerk of *nisi prius* return th[e] Postea, or shew
cause why an Attachment sho[uld] not Issue against him.—

After the Rule for Judgment is out the Party in whose Favor it is, carries
the Record to the Judge who inserts of increase and signs Judgment in the
Margin of the Roll thus "Judgment sign[ed] the   Day of
MDCCLXXXVII A.B." Note the Plaintiff must previously give 4 Days
Notice of taxing Costs & serve Defendant with a Copy of the Bill.

The Plaintiff may amend his Declaration any Time in the first Term
before Issue join[s] without leave of the Court, but after the first Term or
Issue joined he must apply to the Court for Leave.—

In Matter merely of Form the Court will grant Leave without Costs, but
in Matter of Substance he must pay Costs.—

---

[18] Jeofails, 32 Hen 8, c. 30 (1540); 18 Eliz 1, c. 14 (1575).

EDITOR'S NOTES TO *Practical Proceedings* . . .

1.   The Bill of Middlesex was a precept which issued from the English Court of King's Bench.[a] As noted above, by ordinances of colonial New York's Governors Bellomont[b] and Cornbury,[c] the New York Supreme Court of Judicature had cognizance of all pleas which in England could be heard in the Courts of Exchequer, Common Pleas, and King's Bench. Consequently this New York court had its choice of forms of process, and for first process used both the Common Pleas *capias* and King's Bench Bill of Middlesex.[d] This bill directed the sheriff of the county in which the court sat to bring a defendant before the court to answer a fictitious plea of trespass. Once the defendant was in the custody of the court or had given bail, by the ancient privilege *ratione loci* he could be declared against for the real cause of action. If the defendant were in another county, King's Bench would issue a writ of latitat to the sheriff there, commanding him to bring the party before the court, also to answer a fictitious plea of trespass. This procedural device extended the legitimate jurisdiction which King's Bench had over actions of trespass to include the actions of debt, detinue, account, and covenant—actions which previously were within the exclusive jurisdiction of Common Pleas. This provided financial and procedural advantages to a plaintiff that were not available at Common Pleas, and by the middle of the seventeenth century it had become the usual manner of commencing a civil action.[e] Although with one court performing the functions of Common Pleas and King's Bench in New York it was not necessary to use two different types of process, such was the practice, and it was continued by the court when the colony achieved independence. After the New York State Supreme Court sat in both New York City and Albany, the bill was alternatively a Bill of New York or a Bill of

---

[a] 1 Crompton, *Practice of Common Pleas* (2d ed. 1783) 9.

[b] An Ordinance for Establishing Courts of Judicature &c., in 2 *NY Laws* (Van Ness and Woodworth Rev. 1813), Appendix x-xii.

[c] An Ordinance for Further Establishing the Supreme Court of Judicature &c., in 2 *NY Laws* (Van Ness and Woodworth Rev. 1813), Appendix xiii-xiv.

[d] Livingston, William, *Lawyers' Book of Precedents* (Ms. NYSL c. 1760); Wyche, *NY Supreme Court Practice* (2d ed. 1794) 41.

[e] 1 Holdsworth, *History of English Law* (1922) 199-200; Hale, "A Discourse Concerning the Courts of King's-Bench and Common-Pleas," in Hargrave, *A Collection of Tracts* (1787) 363-367.

Albany. This was in imitation of the English rule that if King's Bench sat in a county other than Middlesex, the bill took the name of the county where the court was in fact sitting when the action was brought. The similarity of a Bill of Albany and a Bill of Middlesex is illustrated in Exhibit A.

2.   The writ of *capias* was based upon a fictitious writ of trespass *quare clausum fregit*[f] and was used as first process in the English Court of Common Pleas. Resort to the fiction was to help Common Pleas to compete with King's Bench by avoiding the cost of an original writ. Like a Bill of Middlesex, it directed the sheriff to have the defendant before the court on a certain day. The characteristics which distinguished it from a Bill of Middlesex were that it was issued in the name of the King, and that it was tested or witnessed by the chief justice of the court rather than merely signed by the clerk; thus it was a writ and not a precept.[g]

Hamilton was not technically accurate, for in New York a *capias* was not the *only* first process which could be used when a defendant resided in another county. In imitation of English King's Bench practice, a latitat (see Exhibit C) based upon the fictitious return of a nonexistent bill could serve this purpose.[h] Examination of early New York writs and lawyers' records casts some light upon the manner in which the New York Supreme Court adopted the process of two English courts to do essentially the same task. Apparently the usual practice was to use a bill if the defendant resided within the county where the court was sitting and to use a *capias* in most other situations.

A case from William Smith's *Ms. Register A*[i] provides a striking example of this, and at the same time illustrates the lack of understanding on the part of New York practitioners for the function these two types of process served in their respective courts in England. In the 1752 case of *Sontas v. Dowe and Bayard* joint defendants lived in different cities, Dowe in New York where the court was sitting, and Bayard in Albany. Smith notes in his register that on the same day he issued a Bill of New York for defendant Dowe, and a *capias* to the sheriff of Albany for defendant Bayard. If strict King's Bench process

---

[f] See "Editor's Note" 3, *infra,* at p. 65.
[g] 1 Crompton, *Practice of Common Pleas* (2d ed. 1783) 9.
[h] Boote, *Treatise* (1781) 15; Wyche, *NY Supreme Court Practice* (2d ed. 1794) 44, 45.
[i] Ms. NYPL.

had been used, a bill would have issued in New York City and a latitat would have been sent to Albany. If Common Pleas process had been used, a *capias* would have been directed to the sheriffs of both cities.

With English process being used in New York Colony in this manner, it is quite possible that at the time Hamilton was writing (in 1782) it was not the practice for a latitat to be used as first process into another county, and therefore Hamilton may not have been in error when he stated that for this purpose "first process *must* be a *capias*. . . ."[j]

3. Hamilton's statement that a New York *capias* is a "Writ compounded of the Capias of Common Pleas and Bill of Middlesex of the King's Bench" is repeated nearly verbatim in DeWitt Clinton's *Ms. Precedent Book* (c. 1787), and is paraphrased in 1794 by Wyche, who wrote that a *capias* was ". . . a writ compounded of that used in the English common pleas, and the bill of New-York. . . ."[k] None of these statements is accurate, for a New York *capias* was nearly identical to that used in Common Pleas in the reign of George III.[l] It is probable that Wyche relied upon *Practical Proceedings* for his description of the New York *capias*. At page ix of his preface to *New York Supreme Court Practice* (2d ed. 1794) Wyche states, "Some practical sketches in manuscript, one passing under the name of a personage of high respectability, have been consulted. . . ." It appears that this personage was Hamilton. Furthermore, although *Practical Proceedings* is not referred to in Clinton's volume, it is a logical source for this repeated error.

An understanding of the nature of the *capias* used in New York requires some knowledge of the development of the writ of *capias* in Common Pleas. Originally a defendant could not be arrested and imprisoned on first process in a purely civil action if no force had been alleged, and plaintiffs had to coerce their opponents into court by the cumbersome process of attachment and distress. Because of the unfair delays this caused, a series of enactments beginning in the second half of the thirteenth century authorized use of the *capias* for actions of account, debt, detinue, and covenant.[m] Eventually in

---

[j] (Emphasis added.) *But see* Wyche, *NY Supreme Court Practice* (2d ed. 1794) 41.

[k] *Ibid.*

[l] See Exhibits B-1, B-2, and B-3.

[m] Hale, "A Discourse Concerning the Courts of King's-Bench and Common-Pleas," in Hargrave, *A Collection of Tracts* (1787) 359 and statutes cited therein.

Common Pleas in order to compete with King's Bench proceedings by bill, the initial purchase of an original writ was omitted and the court would issue a *capias,* founded upon a fictitious original writ of trespass *quare clausum fregit*—the action for trespass upon realty. Resort to a fabricated forceful entry of trespass made it proper for a *capias* to issue. The writ of *capias* recited this trespass, and thus it developed that a fictitious trespass was recited in the *capias* as well as the Bill of Middlesex.[n]

As noted, during the New York colonial period the Supreme Court used both the bill and the *capias* for first process.[o] Although the colonial Bill of New York was practically identical with the Bill of Middlesex, the *capias* was changed slightly, and instead of reciting "to answer a plea wherefore with force and arms he broke the close [QCF]," it merely stated "to answer a plea of trespass, etc. . . ." By 1794 in New York State the "etc." was dropped and the recitation of trespass stated only "to answer a plea of trespass," bringing the recitation of a fictitious trespass in the *capias* to the same form as that in a bill.[p] The salient characteristics of the writ of *capias* were retained, however, with the teste or witness of the chief justice appearing at the end of the writ and with the writ issuing in the name of the king, in the colonial period, and in the name of the people of the state, after New York had achieved independence. The form which the recitation of fictitious trespass took as the writ evolved is illusstrated in Exhibit B.

Thus it appears that a New York State *capias* was a "pure" *capias* which was very similar to that which issued from Common Pleas, and it was not, as Hamilton states, a combination of the latter writ and a Bill of Middlesex or New York. The evolution of the manner of reciting the fictitious trespass in the *capias* and the fact that the New York Supreme Court had the powers of and used the process of the Courts of both King's Bench and Common Pleas seem to have misled Hamilton when he characterized the New York *capias* as "compounded of the Capias of Common Pleas and the Bill of Middlesex of the Kings Bench. . . ."

---

[n] *Id.* at 367; see "Editor's Note" 1, *supra*, at p. 63.

[o] *Supra,* note d.

[p] *Compare* illustrative bills (Exhibits A-1, A-2), *with* illustrations of *capias* (Exhibits B-1, B-2, B-3).

4.   When a *capias* had been returned by a sheriff endorsed that the defendant could not be found in his bailiwick, the plaintiff could procure a *testatum capias*. This writ, directed to the sheriff of the county where the defendant was, stated that it had been testified in court that the defendant would be found there and directed the sheriff to take the man.[q]

5.   In English practice, when a defendant in a civil action had not been taken into custody on an alias and pluries capias, the plaintiff could choose to proceed by writ of exigent to civil outlawry.[r] This procedure was not practiced in the colony or in the state until 1787, when it was legislatively introduced.[s] The dispute over whether plaintiff had to begin his process anew or could continue to issue pluries after pluries perhaps stemmed from the unavailability of the remedy of civil outlawry. Examination of private records of colonial lawyers indicates that pluries after pluries was issued until the defendant was taken into custody.[t]

6.   Analysis of why these English writs were not used indicates that New York lawyers were aware of the implications of a change which had occurred in English law, and took advantage of this change by simplifying New York's jury process while England continued a practice which had become largely unnecessary. Explanation of this interesting development requires some description of the English *nisi prius* system.

Because of the inconvenience of having parties, witnesses, and jurors travel to Westminster for every jury trial, a system was developed whereby, following joinder of issue at bar, suits could be transferred to the country for jury trial of the facts in issue before the circuit justices who customarily heard actions concerning realty at the assizes. The court would issue a writ of *venire facias juratores*, commonly called a *venire*, directing the sheriff to summon jurors to appear at the trial at Westminster, *nisi prius*—unless before the return date the justices of assize came and held the trial in their county. Although the *venire* alternatively directed jurors to be present at Westminster,

---

[q] 1 Crompton, *Practice of Common Pleas* (2d ed. 1783) 21, 22.

[r] 2 Crompton, *op. cit. supra* n. q, at 42.

[s] An Act declaring what Process may be issued in certain personal Actions, and for regulating Outlawries, *NY Laws*, 10th Sess 1787, c. 9 (Greenleaf ed. 1792).

[t] See, e.g., entries for Yalverton v. Curter, in William Wickham's *Supreme Court Register* (Ms. CULL 1768) 6.

it was intended that such trials await arrival of the justices in the country, and so if when the *venire* was returnable the assize justices had not yet come, the *venire* would be continued until the following term, with the anticipation that before then the justices would hold the trial at *nisi prius*, as the court came to be called.

This procedure was attendant with two difficulties. By ancient practice defendants could cast their *essoins* at the return of the *venire*, and so it frequently would happen that when the plaintiff with his witnesses and the sheriff with the panel of jurors were all assembled before the justices, a servant of the defendant would appear with his master's excuse for being absent, and the trial would have to be delayed until the next assize. The other problem was that when jurors were summoned in the same instrument that contained the *nisi prius* clause the first opportunity either party would have to see who was on the panel of jurors was at the trial itself, and no time was afforded to prepare challenges. To remedy these difficulties, it was enacted that except for realty assizes and delivery of jails no jury trials were to be held before the names of all jurors had been turned in to the court at bar.[u]

This effected several changes in the *nisi prius* procedure. The *venire* was made returnable on the last day of the term in which issue was joined, at which time the sheriff would submit the names of the panel of jurors, and the defendant would have to cast his *essoins*. The *venire* still directed that the jurors be summoned to appear at Westminster, but the *nisi prius* clause was dropped from it, and the sheriff, knowing that it was intended for the trial to be held in the county, would not summon the jurors but only take their names. As a tour de force of legal consistency, to rectify procedurally the fictitious default of the jurors who were *not* summoned to appear at bar, the *jurata* of the *nisi prius* roll (the record on which the justices were authorized to hear the trial) would respite them until the following term when they again were to appear at bar, unless first the justices of assize came to the county. Having separated the writ by which the sheriff was directed to select jurors from the writ which also had been used to summon them, it was necessary to devise a new writ for the latter purpose, and it was for this reason that the

---

[u] 3 Blackstone, *Commentaries* (Phila. ed. 1771) 352-354 and statutes therein cited.

English courts used the writs to which Hamilton refers, the *distringas* of King's Bench, and the *habeas corpora juratorum* of Common Pleas.

Thus the *nisi prius* clause in the record for the trial was moved from the *venire* part of the *nisi prius* roll to the *jurata*, and the *nisi prius* clause in the writ to summon jurors was moved from the sheriff's *venire* to the *distringas* or *habeas corpora juratorum*. This contrived English procedure was initiated in 1368 and continued throughout the eighteenth century in spite of the fact that sometime prior to 1738 the casting of *essoins* was no longer permitted in civil actions.[v] The practice was in effect in Colonial New York at least as late as 1746.[w] As Hamilton notes, in post-Revolutionary New York the form of the *jurata* was preserved in the record by respiting the jury until the following term, or until a justice of the court presided at a trial at *nisi prius*.[x] (See Exhibit F.) Since by the English law which the state purported to receive defendants in civil actions could no longer cast *essoins*, there was no longer a reason to use a *distringas* or *habeas corpora juratorum* (loosely termed a habeas corpus in *Practical Proceedings*) to summon jurors, and although these writs were used in the state in certain instances,[y] generally New York practice was to use only one writ, a *venire facias juratores*,[z] thereby returning to the more straightforward English practice of the early fourteenth century. The problem of providing parties with the names of the panel of jurors so that challenges could be prepared was met by having the *venire* issue at least six days prior to the date of the trial, and requiring the sheriff to furnish parties with the names of the jurors within five days of the trial.[aa]

---

[v] See statement of Buller, J., in Argent v. Dean and Chapter of St. Pauls, 3 Doug. 238 (1783).

[w] 3 *Col Laws NY* 599 (1746) (reenacting 3 *Col Laws NY* 185 at 188 [1741]).

[x] Plea and issue roll for ejectment action in James Jackson v. Anthony Post, NY Sup Ct, 784 (Ms. HR).

[y] An Act for the Amendment of the Law, and the better Advancement of Justice, 5 *Col Laws NY* 537, 539 (1773).

[z] Wyche, *NY Supreme Court Practice* (2d ed. 1794) 149, 150.

[aa] *Ibid.*; Hamilton, *Practical Proceedings in the Supreme Court of the State of New York* (Ms. Lib Assoc Bar NYC, c. 1782) [7], [8].

[18]   **BAIL[19]**

When the Cause requires special Bail & Bail has been given in to the Sheriff, if the Defendant neglects to put in special Bail or Bail to the Action within the Time limited by the Rule, the Plaintiff has two Remedies; he may either take an Assignment of the Bail Bond[20] under Seal of the Sheriff in Presence of two Witnesses and sue the Bail or he may have his Remedy against the Sheriff. If he proceeds against the Sheriff he must do it in this Manner; The Term following he must move the Court to this Effect "The Defendant in this Cause having refused to appear according to the Course of the Writ, I pray the Sheriff may bring in the Body within four Days or shew Cause why an Attachment should not Issue," The Court makes a Rule agreeable to this Motion which the Plaintiff must serve upon the Sheriff and he has five Days after Service to have Bail put into the Action After which Time if he has not done it the Plaintiff moves the Court on an Affidavit of Service of the Rule and that no Bail has been put in for an Attachment against the [19] Sheriff the Rule of Court on this is made abso[lute] and an Attachment is issued directed to the Coroner, upon the Return of which the Sheriff is fined at the Discretion of the Court, & commit[ted] until he pays the Fine; the Court on Request order the Fine to be paid to the Plaintiff towa[rd] Satisfaction of his Demand.—

If the Plaintiff takes an Assignment[21] of th[e] Bail Bond and commences his Actions on i[t] the Defendant on Application to the Court may get the Proceedings Staid, but then Ba[il] to the Action must first be put in & Justified in Court leave having been Obtained for that purpose, and then the Court Moved [to] Stay proceedings, which they will do merely by paying Costs, pleading to Issue, receiving a Declaration in the Original Action & tak[ing] Short Notice of Trial if the Plaintiff has not lost a Trial; but if he has lost a Trial they Wi[ll] Oblidge the Parties to consent that Judgme[nt] be entered on the Bail Bond as a security to the Plaintiff and if he in the Course of the Court might have Obtained a [20] Judgment if Bail had been put in,

---

[19] See Exhibit H.
[20] See Exhibit I.
[21] See Exhibit J.

in Time the Court will not stay Proceedings; if the Deft. does not pay Costs the Plaintiff may proceed on the Bail Bond.—

If the Defendant neglects to put in Bail to the Action, and the Bail to the Sheriff want to clear themselves, they must put in Bail to the Action, either themselves or others & then surrender their Principal; they are answerable until Bail is put into the Action and become absolute. When Bail to the Action has first been put in the Plaintiff has 20 Days to[22] except to their Sufficiency, and if he omit to do it in that Time he loses his Right of excepting—The 20 Days are counted from the Time he receives Notice of Bail being put in, The mode of excepting is to go to the person with whom the Bail Piece is lodged, whether Judge or Clerk of the Court & Indorse on the Back of the Bail Piece thus, "I except to the sufficiency of the within Bail Jany. 3d 1785 A.B. Atty" & then immediately give Notice [21] to the other Party that you have excepted the Bail; who must justify the next four Days in Term or the Bail Bond is forfeit[ed]. If the Exception is made in Vacation they may justify before a Judge & send Notice w[ith] a Copy of the Affidavit of Justification to Plaintiffs Attorney; but if the Plaintiff [is] not satisfied with that Justification, th[ey] must Justify in Court, and for this they have four Days in the following Term the Defendant must then take his Bail into Court, and they must make Oath that they are Housekeepers, & each worth double the sum for which they are bou[nd] clear of all Debts or Demands; the Deft. Attorney must give two Days Notice of the Intended Justification to the Plaintiffs Attorney, and if he is not present to acknowledge the Receipt of the Notice an Affidavit must be produced of the Serv[ice] thereof. The Plaintiff may by Affidavit contest the Sufficiency of the Bail as if [22] are Bankrupts &ca. but he must make out the Insufficiency very clear to induce the Court to Refuse their Justification. If the Court thinks his Objection sufficient they will allow the Defendant a Day or two more to add & justify other Bail, After which, if it is not done, the Bail Bond is forfeited; it seems that with Respect to Bail put in before Commissioners in the Country Justification would be Admitted without Oblidging the Bail to appear personally in Court; but if the Plaintiff means to contest it he may Oblige the Defendant to move the Court for Leave for the Bail to Justify upon Affidavit;

---

[22]. *to* inserted with caret in different handwriting.

and he may then dispute their sufficiency as in Case of Bail in Town. It is customary, in order to avoid farther Trouble, to accompany the Notice of Bail with the Copy of the Affidavit of Justification, in Country Causes.—

[Page missing from *Practical Proceedings*; Ms. continues on page 42][23]

[INSERT FROM *Attorney's Practice*]

Bail when bound. [22] When Bail is perfected they become bound that if Judgt. goes against the Deft. he shall pay the Condemnation Money and Costs, or surrender himself in Prison accordingly after Judgt obtained, if he does neither, the Bail are liable; But to make them so, a Ca:Sa: must first [23] issue against the principal, & be returned *non est* & if he lives in another County, a Test: Ca:Sa:

What is requisite to make the Bail liable.

How long the CA, SA. to lie in the Sheriff's Office. There must be at least 8 days between the Test & Return & it must lie 4 Days in the Sheriff's office. It is a doubt whether the Sheriff must endeavour Bonafide to take the principal, or whether the Ca:Sa: is become a matter of form only returnable with a *non Est* at the desire of the plaintiff There are authorities that wear this complexion. The Bail to avail themselves of the Omission must plead it. It must be sued out to charge the Bail, notwithstanding a Writ of Error pending.

Sci Fa, may bear test the return of the Ca.Sa. agt. Prinl. Fifteen days between the Test of the first & second Sci fa. p. 2 Crom. 79.[24]

The Alias *Sci. fa:* must be as teste the day of the return of the first in all cases. ibid.

Every Al: Sci Fa must lie 4 days in Sheriffs office before returnable. ibid.

---

[23] Pages [23]-[24] of our copy of *Practical Proceedings* are missing. We are printing the corresponding pages (22-25) from *Attorney's Practice* (CULL) which present the substance of what probably was in the missing pages. For this purpose, the material will overlap slightly. See also p. 42.

[24] 2 Crompton, *Practice in the Courts of King's Bench and Common Pleas.*

NB. a Ca Sa returnable pending Error, is no regular foundation against the Bail

The Bail may be proceeded against in two ways by Action of Debt upon Recognizance or by [24] Sci fa in Strictness of Law after Ca. sa. returned, The Bail are unconditionably liable; but Courts of Law have indulged them to surrender their principal afterwards; If an Action be bro't on recognizance it is said, the writ must be served 4 days before Return. If an Action of Debt is brought against them they have 8 days in full Term after the writ is returnable to surrender the principle; and if there are not so many in that Term, the residue stand over to the next. If proceeded against by Sci fa: they have, till a Sci, fe. is returned upon the first or a Nihil, upon the second, to make the surrender; and any time on the return day *Sedente Curia.* the surrender will be good. The Sci fa must be 8 days in the Sheriffs office before it is returnable.

(margin) Two ways to proceeds agt. Bail.

(margin) What time Bail has to surrender their Prinl. if Action be bro't on Recoge.

(margin) If Action be bro't on Debt.

(margin) What time they have if proceeded agt. by Sci, Fa.

Note, the Bail are not discharged until the *Exoneretur* is entered on the Bail piece, and they are bound to give immediate notice of the surrender to the plaintiff otherwise they are liable to Costs if for want of knowing it, he proceeds any farther in the suit, and to the consequences of a *Su: persedeas*;[25] if it should take place for want of such notice to enable the plaintiff to charge him in execution.

(margin) Bail to give Notice to the Plaintiff of the Surrender.

The Courts seem lately inclined to charge the Bail to an instance recited in *Burrows Reports*, the warning upon which Sci Fa. was returned, was not given till the very last day, & tho' the Bail offered to make it appear that the warning was served so late as to put it out of their power to surrender this principal before they did

(margin) 3. Burr. 1360[26]

[25] See Exhibit K.
[26] Hunt v. Coxe, 3 Burr. 1360 (KB 1763).

(to wit on the same night) Yet [25] the Court refused to go into an investigation of the matter, saying it was the duty of the Bail to have searched the Sheriffs Office to Know whether the Sci, fa. had been lodged there or not.

When two are bail altho' *one* be in Execution, the plaintiff may take the *other* Jac. L D.[27] 2 Cro. 320.[28] 2d Bulst. 68."[29]

[End of Insert]

[*Practical Proceedings* continues]

[25] before they did, (it was on the same Night) yet the Court refused to go into an Investigation of the Matter, and said it was the Duty of the Bail to search the Sheriffs Office to know whether the Sci: fa: had been lodged there or not.—

The Scire facias must be in the Sheriffs office eight Days before the Return.—

If the Principal dies any Time before the Ca:sa: is returnable the Bail are discharged but if he dies any Time After, not surrendered they are liable without Remedy.—

The Bail may take their Principal without Warrant, but they cannot in this Case delegate their Custody of him without his consent in Writing, they may even take him on a Sunday & surrender him the next Day.—

The Manner of surrendering is this The Bail go with their Principal and the Sheriff or his Bailiff to a Judges Chamber, & there in his presence of the Judge they [26] Deliver their Principal to the Sheriff, & pray the Judge to enter an *Exoneratur* upon the Bail Piece thus, "The within named A.B. has surrendered himself in Discharge of his Bail this 13th Day of Jany. 1785.[30] R.M."—

A Copy of this *Reddit. se* may be a Warrent to the Officer, to keep him in Custody; the Bail are not Discharged until the *Exonerator* is entered on the

---

[27] Jacob, *A New Law Dictionary* (7th ed. 1756), tit. Bail, citing 2 Cro. 320 and 2 Bulst. 68 for the proposition.

[28] Higgens Case, Cro. Jac. 320 (KB 1613).

[29] Higgins v. Sommerland, 2 Bulst. 68 (KB 1613). End of substitution from *Attorney's Practice*. See n. 23, *supra*.

[30] See p. 41 and n. 14, *supra*.

Bail Piece, And they are Bound to give Immediate Notice to the Plaintiffs Attorney; otherwise they are liable to Costs, if for want of knowing it he proceeds any farther in the suit and to the Consequence of a Supersedeas, if it should take place for want of such Notice: to Enable the Plaintiff to charge the Prisoner in Execution after a Ca:sa: returned It is necessary, to make the surrender a good one, that the Principal should be two Days in Custody; if he is rescued or escapes before that [27] the Bail are still liable, tho' I imagine they might have a Remedy against the Sheriff if he was once in Prison.—

The most accurate Rule with respect to holding the Defendant to special Bail seems to be this when the Cause of Action arises upon some thing of an ascertainable Value, where the Plaintiff can with propriety swear to his Damages there Bail is of Course; but where Damages are of an uncertain Nature and to be assessed *ad libitum,* by the Jury, there Bail cannot be demanded of Course; in this Case a Judges Order must be Obtained which he grants at Discretion according to the Apparent Importance of the Case.—

The general Rule is against Bail of Course in Trespass, either because the Quantum of the Injury is uncertain, or there is some Aggravation arising from the Force, which cannot be ascertained but by the Jury, it is said in Barnes,[31] Bail is of Course in Debt; however an Act of Assembly allows it of Cours[e] [28] in some Cases of *Trespass quare clausum fregit, Detinue, Trover & Assumpsit;*[32] but the Doctrine is one of those which are involved in the uncertainty of contradictory Divisions.—

It was omitted in its proper place that if the first Bail was doubtful the Deft. may add other Bail, include them in the Notice of Justification and let them justify at the Time proposed for the first

---

[31] LeWrit v. Tolcher, Barnes (1790 ed.) 79 (CP 1739).

[32] An Act to discourage Tortious Entries and Possessions, 5 *Col Laws NY* 786 (1775). While this statute refers only to trespass *quare clausum fregit,* Hamilton's statement appears to encompass also detinue, trover, and assumpsit. Comparison with Hamilton, *Attorney's Practice* (1802) and Wyche, *NY Supreme Court Practice* (2d ed. 1794) indicates that the above statement of the law may be misleading. *Attorney's Practice* at pages 26-27 states: "However an Act of the Legislature allows it of Course in some cases of Trespass QUARE CLAUSUM FREGIT, much more ought it to be of Course in Trespass DE BONIS ASPORTATIS, it is of Course in Debt, Detinue Trover and Assumpsit." According to Wyche at pages 29-30, in an action of trover defendant may be held to bail of course because "this is more an action of property, than a *tort.*" In assumpsit, he asserted, the damages may be reduced to a certainty and special bail is demandable of course. It seems reasonable that, by parity of reasoning, special bail was available of course in detinue.

wrong   *There is no special Bail in actions on Penal Statutes*, nor in Covenant
unless for non payment of Money, nor in Debt upon Bond to per-
form Covenants; but with Regard to the Damages by the Breach, the
Measure of which shall be taken from the Plaintiffs Oath, nor in Account
until Judgment *quod computet* nor in Battery.—

When any of your Bail happen to be material Witnesses you must make
an Affidavit of the Fact in the Usual Terms, [29] and having sufficient
Sureties, you may move the Court for Leave to put in the other Bail in their
Place and have them released, which will be granted. It will be proper to give
the Plaintiff the previous Notice usual upon such Motions; this may be done
on the Day of Trial the Bail must enter into a Recognizance & Justify at the
same Time in Court.

You cannot hold to special Bail Heirs Executors or Administrators in any
suit against them for which the Testator was liable, or Ancestor, nor can you
hold to Bail Members of the Legislature. while serving.

salk.   Where the Defendant in an Action has put in special Bail and
98.99.[33] the Plaintiffs neglects to Declare in two Terms, the Defendant upon
Affidavit and Notice of Motion may get himself discharged within
the third Term on a Common Appearance, unless Plaintiff should Declare
before [30] Motion made which I apprehend would bar the Motion. vide
Bacon.—[34]

If the Defendant be Imprisoned for want of common Bail, and before the
Return of the Writ he has it in his power to procure Bail the Sheriff may
admit him to Bail at his pleasure; but if the Sheriff Refuses to Release him on
Bail or he cannot Procure Bail till the Sheriff has Returned the Writ, he must
put in good Bail and move the Court to be Discharged from his confinement,
& that a Supersedeas Issue to the Sheriff for that purpose. I see no Reason
why the Defendant may not be Released in this Manner any time during the
Action; some have been of Opinion that a *Habeas Corpus*, to bring the
Defendant before one of the Judges in Vacation in Order to be Admitted to
Bail is a proper Proceeding, but it is doubted by the generality of the
Practisers here, who hold that the Party shall [31] have no Remedy but on

---

[33] Holland v. Serjeant, 1 Salk 98 (1698 KB).

[34] 1 Bacon, *A New Abridgment of the Law* (3d ed. 1768) 213.

Application to the Court as above.[35] It must be Remembered that a Supersedeas in this Case issues in order to indemnify the Sheriff against a *Non est* returned to Ca:sa: against Defendant.—

When the Defendant is arrested on a Writ with *an ac etiam*^ the proper Remedy is to move the Court Immediately after the Return of the Writ that the Plaintiff shew Cause of Action; which is done by mak- **& the Deft. disputes the legality of it[36]** ing Affidavit of his Demand. The Rule obtained in Consequence of this Motion, should be served on the Plaintiff; and till it is complied with the Defendant is under no Necessity to put in *special Bail.*—

When Bail is put in *before,* or *on* the Continuance Day of a Term it is filed as of the preceding Term, when After, as of the Subsequent; but when Bail are added, it shall be filed as of the Term the first Bail was put in.—

[32] If a Defendant be arrested by a wrong Name he need not Join in the Recognizance of Bail and then he will not be preclueded from pleading *Misnomer,* otherwise he will. (Salkeld.)[37]

If Plaintiff once takes an Assignment of the Bail Bond, and the Defendant takes the usual Steps to stay proceedings, and the Bail below become Bail above, the Plaintiff cannot except to them

The Sheriff may take Bail in double the sum mentioned in the Ac etiam, but the Bail are only liable to that sum & Costs.—Salk 102.[38]

The Sheriff is obliged to take Reasonable Bail & if he refuses sufficient Bail he is liable to an Action on the Case; if he utterly Refuses to take Bail at all he is liable to an Action of false Imprisonment. The Sheriff may take Bail on an Attachment *pro pace,* not on one for Contempt.—

----

[35] The "generality of the Practisers" had the authorities on their side. Unless New York's jurisprudence had developed an unrecorded innovation in the application of the writ of habeas corpus, it appears that a supersedeas and not a habeas corpus was the proper writ with which a prisoner in this situation could gain his release. I Richardson, *Attorney's Practice in the Court of Common Pleas* (4th ed. 1796) 297; 14 Viner, *A General Abridgment of Law and Equity* (1st ed. 1742) 216; 2 Lilly, *The Practical Register or a General Abridgment of the Law* (2d ed. 1735) 3; 4 Bacon, *A New Abridgment of the Law* (3d ed. 1768) 670.

[36] This marginal note is in a different band but appears to have been added by the same person who added the interlineations and marginal notations at pp. [86], [107], [108], [113]. This person is hereafter cited as person "A."

[37] Anonymous, 2 Salk 519 (KB 1702).

[38] Genbaldo v. Cognoni, 1 Salk 102 (KB 1705). This notation was apparently made by person "A." See n. 36, *supra.*

[33]   ATTORNEYS

They cannot be held to Special Bail & must be prosecuted in the Courts to which they belong; if an Action is commenced against him in any other, they can stay it by Writ of Privilege.—

But their Privilege extends only to where they sue alone, and in their own Right. The Process against them commences by a Declaration Thus, A complains against B one of the Attornies of the Court of the People now here present for this, to wit, &c" as in other Cases.

This peculiarity in the Form runs throughout all the Proceedings. He can only be proceeded against in Term Time, *sedente curia*

An Attorney when he is Plaintiff has a Writ called an Attachment of Privilege.—[39]

No Attorney can be lessee in Ejectment, nor can he be Bail in the Court to which he belongs if an Attorney neglects to plead in Time he may be forejudged of his Privilege [34] and you may then take out a Capias against him & hold him to Bail.—The Rule I believe is, "That he plead in 20 Days or be forejudged of his Privilege, Note, you conclude your Declaration against an Attorney thus, "And therefore he prays Relief &c."—Instead of the common Form.—

[35]   VENUE

The Venue is the *Visne* or Neighbourhood in which the Cause of Action arose and this must be specified in the Declaration; in all local Actions as, Ejectment, quare clausum fregit, concerning the Customs of the place &c: the Venue must be laid in the Declaration, where the Cause of Action arose; there are other Actions where the same is applicable, as Escape, *false Return,* and all Actions against Officers relative to their Office; transitory Actions the Plaintiff may at his option lay where he pleases; there are some others which must be laid in their proper Counties. By transitory Actions are understood,

---

[39] See Exhibit L.

those which might have arisen as well in one place as another, and in the Merits of which the locality of the Action has no Share; this is Applicable to most contracts & Torts relative to Personalities: however it is very often in the Power of the Defendant when the [36] Venue is laid out of the County in which the Cause of Action arose, to have it changed by moving the Court on an Affidavit, that Cause of Action, if any arose not in the County where Plaintiff laid it, but in another County, specifying it, and not in any other Place out of the said County. To this there are many Exceptions, the Court will in no case of *Specialty, Priviledge or Promissory Note,** change the Venue laid in the Declaration; nor will they do it in any Action if the Plaintiff will undertake that some Evidence material to the Issue, does actually arise in the County where the Venue is laid, but he must be careful how he undertakes this, for if there is not some Evidence really material to the Issue produced there he will be nonsuited.

[37] The Court exercise a very discretionary Power with respect to the Venue & will change it whenever it can be made appear, that Substantial Justice cannot be held in the County where it is laid, of this there are many Exempts.—

In an Action founded on a Lease the Venue may be laid either where the Lease was made or where the land lies, as against the Lessee, but with Respect to the Assignees of the Lessee it must be laid where the Land lies.—

After Venue changed by the Defendant, he cannot plead in Abatement. The Defendant must move to have the Venue changed before Plea pleaded, and the Plaintiff—when he opposes it must do it before Replication.—

The Plaintiff cannot professedly change his Venue, but he may do it in Effect by moving to amend, any Time during   2 Str:1162-1202[41] the first Term but not Afterwards.—

An Attorney has Priviledge to lay his Venue in all Actions where the Court Sits.

---

* Venue may be changed on Promissory Note. Wilson 173—[40]

[40] Hallett v. Hallett, 1 Wils 173 (KB 1747).

[41] Stroud v. Tilly, 2 Str. 1162 (KB 1742), cited as authority in Rivet et al. v. Cholmondley et al., 2 Str. 1202 (KB 1744).

[38]   WARRANTS OF ATTORNEY

Regularly both Plaintiff & Defendant ought to give Warrants of Attorney to their Attornies, which each should enter upon his Register & Dogget. These Warrants of Attorney should precede the Memorandum on the Issue & Judgment Rolls; that for the Plaintiff must be inserted in the Declaration immediately after Pledges of Prosecution and that for Defendant after the Plea; it is often neglected to take Warrants of Attorney, but it is rather dangerous for the Want of them would be Error & abate the Action upon a special Demurrer.—Warrants of Attorney to confess Judgment are of Different kinds sometimes they are Inserted

[*Marginal addition:*]

in a Bond when Originally given some times they are afterwards given to confess Judgment. Note by stat.[42] bond. & warrt. of Atty. must be separate—

It may be acted upon at any time; if it is given to confess Judgment of any particular Term" (without adding "or any subsequent Term") it will not authorize a Confession in any other Term; it may in fact be given in [39] Vacation to confess Judgment of the Preceding Term, but it must be dated in that Term. The Manner of proceeding is this, The Attorney who is to confess Judgment must file common Bail as in another Case, receive a Declaration and either confess the Action, or let Judgment go by *nihil dicit* or *non sum informatus*, the Roll must be made up accordingly & Judgment signed; this may be done in Vacation as well as Term & if the Warrant is to confess Judgment of any particular Term, and the Party dies any Day before the Day in Bank of the Subsequent Term, Judgment may be entered as of the Preceding Term. If four Terms have elapsed without confessing Judgment it cannot be done without Motion to the Court founded on Affidavit setting forth, that the Parties are living, that the Warrant was duly executed, and that the Debtor part thereof [40] remains unsatisfied; if Twenty years have elapsed it cannot be done till after a Rule to shew Cause has been given.—

---

[42] The statute referred to is An Act for the Amendment of the Law and the better Advancement of Justice, *NY Laws*, 11 Sess 1788, c. 46, sec. 24. While the handwriting appears to be the same as the rest of the manuscript, this gloss was probably added by the transcriber to bring his copy up to date after he had completed it. See p. 41 and n. 14, *supra*.

A Warrant of Attorney given by a Person in Custody on ~~profits~~ mesne process to confess Judgment on the Debt or Demand of the Party at whose suit he is arrested is not valid unless an Attorney is present in Behalf of the Prisoner to explain the nature of the Act to him and witness the Execution; but it may be given to a third person without this, vide I Salk. 402.[43] If a Person is in Custody he may give a Warrant of Attorney to confess Judgment to a Person becoming Bail for him; without the Presence of an Attorney; If he is in Custody on final Process the Presence of an Attorney on his Behalf is not necessary for he must at all Events gain by it, by [41] respecting his confinement and the Satisfaction he is bound to make.—

If a Warrant of Attorney be given to a *Feme sole* and she afterwards marries, you cannot enter Judgment without Leave of the Court. Warrants of Attorney to confess Judgment are not revokeable the Authority Determines with the Death of the Party. If given by a *Feme sole,* and she marries before Judgment the Warrant is countermanded. I Show. 91.[44] I Salk. 171.[45] the authorities differ as to the Marriage being a countermand.—

[42]   PLEAS

Pleas are divided into two kinds, in abatement & in Bar, and the last into general and special Pleas.—

Pleas in Abetement are to the Jurisdiction of the Court, to the Disability of the Plaintiff, or to some Defect or Informality in the Writ or Declaration, or to a Variance between them.

Formerly there was a great deal of nice Learning about Pleas in abetement, which is now in Little Estimation and indeed the Pleas themselves are seldom used; and are always discountenanced by the Court, which having lately acquired a more liberal Cast begin to have some faint Idea that the end of Suits at Law is to Investigate the Merits of the Cause, and not to entangle in the Nets of technical Terms. The General Doctrine seems to be as follows,

---

[43] Anonymous, 1 Salk 402 (KB 1704).
[44] Nightingale v. Adams, 1 Show. 91 (KB 1690).
[45] Anonymous, 1 Salk 171 (KB 1702).

You Plead to the Jurisdiction of the Court, [43] when the Action is of such a Nature of which it has not properly Cognizance or when it is Arisen out of its Jurisdiction; this Plea must be pleaded before Imparlance, and in Person not by Attorney for by Demanding an Imparlance you Acknowledge the Jurisdiction of the Court; it asserts that the Plaintiff ought not have or maintain his Action[46] because &ca. and Concludes praying Judgment, whether the Court will have further Cognizance of the Matter.—

Note I imagine it means before you ask a special Imparlance. 3 Blackstone 301.[47] here also you must make but half Defence, Stopping at Injury without adding *when and where* &c.

A Plea to Disability of the Person is when the Plaintiff is Feme Covert, Infant outlawed excommunicated or under any [44] legal Disability for Carrying on a Suit at Law; this concludes with praying Judgment whether you ought to answer the Plaintiffs Bill. A Plea to the Writ or Declaration prays Judgment of the Writ or Bill and that the same may be quashed It seems you must pray Judgment of the Declaration, for this Form has been adjudged to belong to a Plea in Bar, however this Distinction is to me not so Intelligiable. after a Bail Bond is forfeited and the Proceedings Stayed by the Court you cannot Plead in Abatement of the Original Action. A Plea in Bar is where you totally Deny the Matter alledged in the Declaration and this Amounts to the *general Issue*,[48] or you Oppose some special Matter which tends to overthrow the Facts, or Distroy the Right of Action [45] founded upon them. It is a general Rule that you cannot Plead a special Plea which in reality amounts to the General Issue only.—

A Stranger to a Bond cannot Plead *non est factum*,[49] but *rien ne passa par le fait,* nothing passed by the Deed.—

The General Rule when to Plead *non est factum* is, when the Deed is the Immediate foundation of the Action, and some Matter *in pais* is only Inducement to it; as in a Bond the Acknowledgment of the Debt in the Penalty is the Immediate foundation of the Action, the nonperformance of

---

[46] It is not possible to determine whether the owner of the manual made the insertion of *his Action* or whether it was done by another person.

[47] 3 Blackstone, *Commentaries* (1771 ed.) 301.

[48] For plea to the general issue in trepass, see Exhibit M.

[49] See Exhibit N. For plea of *nil debet,* see Exhibit O. For plea of *non assumpsit,* see Exhibit P.

the Condition is only a Collateral Circumstance that enables you to act upon the first. In Debt for Rent it is said the Lease only leads to the Incurring the Debt, the [46] Subsequent Entry & Enjoyment of the Lessee produces or generates the Debt, and is the Immediate Foundation of the Action.—

Replevin is a Peculiar Action were both Parties are in a certain Sence *Actors* or Plaintiff, and the Defendant, if he may be so Called, makes Avoury or Cognizance; by the first he avows the taking of the Goods, but Justifies on some Ground of Right, this is where he hath acted in his own or the Right of his Wife; by the second he Acknowledges the taking and Justifies as Bailiff or Sarvant in the Command of some Person who has a Right; this is when he really Acted as Bailiff or Sarvant; the Issue on this Action is *Non-Cepit*, which puts the mere taking in Issue.—

[47] *Solvit ad diem* is sometimes ranked among general Issues, but is more properly a special Plea & is in the Form of one; you may by Statute Plead Payment After the Day "According to the Form of the Statute" &c:[50] And the Plea will be good. Under either of these Pleas you may give in evidence not only Actual Payment, but the Omission of Payment of any Rent, or any Part, of Principal or Interest within 20 Years (or there abouts) preceding, which amounts to a violent Presumption of Payment; but you must take care which of the two you use According to Circumstances; if there has been no Payment at all from the Time the Money became due within twenty years, you then plead payment at the Time the last [48] Payment was made, and the Subsequent omission for Twenty years will validate your Plea—

Special Pleas are of endless Variety and Intricacy and appertain to Counsel Business. The distinguishing Form of them is this "And says that the said B. ought not to have or maintain his said Action against him because he says, "here alledge whatever your Plea is built upon," and this he is Ready to verify, wherefore he prays Judgment whether the said B Ought to have or maintain his said Action against him."—[51]

The principal Characteristics of Special Pleading are these, they ought to be single direct and positive, not argumentative, having Convenient Certainty

---

[50] An Act for the amendment of the Law, and the better advancement of Justice, 5 *Col Laws NY* 540 (1773).

[51] See plea in Rutgers v. Waddington, printed at pp. 320-328, *infra*.

of Time place and person, answering all the Substantial [49] Parts of the Plaintiffs Declaration. But now by Statute[52] with leave of Court, you may plead as many special Pleas as you think proper; the Practice with us is to plead as many as you think necessary for your Defance without previously applying for Leave, and if the Opposite Party thinks any of them exceptionable he takes a Judges Summons and Requires you to appear and shew Cause why certain of your Pleas should not be struck out, and when you attend the Judge, if you cannot Satisfy him that they ought all to Stand, he will order you to Strik out part of them, but it is at your Election which to reject, or which to Retain. It is said the Power given to the Court is to prevent contradictory Pleas, but you often see in authorized Precedents, Pleas altogether inconsistent with each other, but this is among [50] the Absurdities with which the Law abounds.—

It is impossible to fix certain Rules when you may give the special Matter in Evidance on the General Issue, however this General Observation may be made, that you may give in Evidence whatever goes to the *Gist of the Matter put in Issue.*—

In Debt on *non est Factum* whatever tends to prove that the Bond was Forged, was not duly executed, was void in the Beginning, or avoided afterwards, may be given in Evidence, other Matters must be specially pleaded.—

In Trespass you must generally plead the special Matter, for on the general Issue you can only disprove the Facts alledged "the taking and carrying away," breaking the Close &c:—

In many Actions on the Case you have [51] greater Latitude, but in some of them you are more Confined, espatially in Actions for Words yet even in this you may in Mitigation of Damages give Special Matter to shew that there was no Malice, and that the words were not Intended in the sence in which they were taken, but not to prove the Truth of them, this latter must be pleaded.—

In Trover you may give almost any thing in Evidence on the general Issue; and it is said by Bathurst Introduction to Trials at Nisi prius,[53] that he hardly new more than two special Pleas in Trover, *Release & payment.*—

---

[52] 5 *Col Laws NY* 538 (1773).
[53] Bathurst, *Introduction to the Law Relative to Trials at Nisi Prius* (1768) 45, 46.

In Assumpsit you have almost as general Latitude; it is said: by Bathurst, that you may give any thing in Evidence Either to shew there was nothing originally due or that it was Afterwards discharged [52] he excepts however such Matters of positive Law as avoid the Debt tho' originally just, The Statute of Limitations for Instance, which must be specially pleaded.—

Some other authorities however, take a Distinction they say that in an Assumpsit in Deed you must plead payment, in an Assumpsit in Law you must give it in Evidence on the general Issue; but Gilberts *Prac: Comn: Pleas*[54] says that the Gist of this Action is some Fraud or Delusion in not performing your Promise, and whatever proves no Promise made or broken may be given in Evidence.—

In Covenant I believe you must pretty strictly plead the special Matter.—

In Detinue you must do the same, except the Mere Part of the Taking &c. and for this you plead *non Cepit*.—

[53] In Ejectment you give everything in Evidence on the General Issue; the Books speak of special Pleas, but what they say, on the present Plan is unintelligible; for by the Common Rule you are bound to plead the general Issue; perhaps the special Pleas spoken of were in Use before the Action Assumed its present Form.—Note, At common Law Although you could not plead double, you might by a *Protastando* deny one thing and specially plead another, called by Coke an Exclusion of a Conclusion.—[55]

Demurrer, is an Issue at Law, by which you acknowledge the Truth of the Facts that are Sufficiently Stated, and Question the Law arising from them; this is done in the Following Form. [54] "And the said A says that the Matter contained in the said Declaration Of the said B, for the Matter by the said B above in pleading alledged (or in the Replication &c as the case may be) are in no wise sufficient in Law for him the said B to have & maintain his said Action against the said A; Neither hath he need or is he bound by the Law, *by the Law* of the Land to answer to the said Declaration (Plea &c as the Case may be) and this he is Ready to verify; wherefore for want of Sufficient

54 Gilbert, *History and Practice of the Court of Common Pleas* (1761) 64.
55 1 Coke, *Institutes* *124b.

Declaration &c: on this Behalf he prays Judgment and that the said A may go thereof without a Day."—[56]

"And the said B says that the Matter above by him in his said Declaration (or as the case may be) alledged are good & Sufficient to maintain the said [55] Action of the said B against the said A and this he is Ready to verify; Wherefore and for as much as the said A has in no wise denied the Matters by the said B above in his Declaration &c. alledged no[r] has said anything in Bar or Preclusio[n] of the Action of the said B the said B prays Judgment and that his Debt and Damages aforesaid may be adjudged to him."[57]

This is not accurate but it is Substantially the Form.—

The Parties Generally agree upon a Written State of Facts to prevent Controversy. When the Parties have joined in Demurrer they make up Paper Books, The Plaintiff Delivers one to the Chief Justice and to the Senior Judge; the Paper Books Contain the History of the Proceeding in Nature of Issue Rolls. When this i[s] [56] done the Plaintiff moves the Court that the Paper Books may be entered on Record, and made a *Consilium*, the Court appoint a Day to give Judgment, which is meant by the Motion; the Manner of entering the Continuances is, by *Curia advisare vult*. The Parties in the mean Time exhaust the Arguments on both Sides, and these are Delivered to the Court, who consider them, and give Judgment accordingly. Demurrers must be signed by Counsel.—

When you plead an Abatement founded upon Matter of Fact, you must make an Affidavit of the Truth and shew probable Cause.

When a Plea in Abatement is over Ruled on Demurrer there is a *Respondeas Ouster*; but when it comes to Issue of Fact & Trial it is peremtory.—

[57] After Imparlance whether general or Special, *semper paratus* is no Plea, because by Craving an Imparlance, it appears he was not *semper paratus* Carth. 413.—[58]

If there is a Demurrer to Part, and an Issue upon the other Part and Judgment is given for the Plaintiff on the Demurrer he may enter a non pross as to the Issue and proceed to a Writ of Inquiry on the Demurrer, but with-

---

[56] See also demurrer in Rutgers v. Waddington, printed *infra* at pp. 329-330.

[57] See also joinder in demurrer in Rutgers v. Waddington, printed *infra* at pp. 330-331.

[58] Giles v. Hart, Carth. 413 (KB 1698).

out a Nonpross he cannot have a Writ of Inquiry; because on the Trial of Issue the same Jury will ascertain the Damages for that Part of which the Demurrer was. Salk. 219. pl. 6.[59] If there is a Demurrer to Part and an Issue as to the other Part, the Issue generally stays till the Demurrer is argued.—

[58]   ## PLEAS PUIS DAREIN CONTINUANCE

This is When in the Progress of an Action an Event happens of which the Party may avail himself to abate or bar the Action, as if a feme sole Plaintiff should marry; but in this Case the Party must take Advantage of it at the next Continuance, that is at the commencement of the next Term, for by a Continuance is meant the Interval between the last of one Term to the Beginning of the next; if he does not take Advantage of it at the next Continuance he will be foreclosed and driven to his *Audita querela*. When the Defendant makes use of this Plea, he stakes all upon it; for it Implyedly Acknowledges the Plaintiffs Right of Action previously, and Relies wholly upon itself to defend it; if it is determined against the Defendant [59] it is peremptory & final. The Court must be moved to Plead it upon Affidavit setting forth that since the last Continuance such an Event happened; the Plea runs thus, when in Bar; And the said B comes & defends "the force and Injury when &c: and says that the said A ought not to have or maintain his said Action, because he says that since the last Continuance &c. wherefore he prays Judgment, whether the said A ought to have and maintain his said Action"—You must be very particular in this Plea to specify the Day and Place the Event happened upon which your Plea is founded. 2 Bathurst 438.[60] It is at the Discretion of the Court to allow this Plea or not If it is produced at *nisi prius* and allowed it must be Returned as Part of the *Postea* for the Plaintiff cannot reply at the Assizes [60] nor has the Judge there any Power to accept this Replication and proceed on the Trial; his Authority is only to Try Issues joined in the Court above. idem 139. This Plea may be pleaded any

[59] Anonymous, 1 Salk 219 (KB 1702).

[60] 2 Bathurst, *Introduction to the Law Relative to Trials at Nisi Prius* (1768 ed.) 292. "Idem 139," below, should probably read "idem 439." See *Attorney's Practice* (1802) 52.

Time before Verdict given and After the Jury have gone from the Bar. It is
Peremptory against Defendant even in Abatement.

[61]   PROFERT IN CURIA

When a Specialty is the foundation of the Action or is introduced in the
Course of Pleading it is necessary in many Cases to make a Profert of it to the
Court; the Form of Words used to this purpose, after setting forth the
Instrument you add, "And to the Court of the People now here shewn," agreeable to which you must have the Deed ready for the Inspection of the Court;
the Design of this is that the Court may see that the Deed has the necessary
Marks of authenticity, and the prescribed legal Solemnities. The Rules laid
down when a Profert in Curia is necessary are these;—When it is the immediate Foundation of, or Gist of the Action, Plea &c.—But when it is introduced collaterally, or in Aid it is not necessary to make a Profert.—

[62] When the Matter of the Deed lies in *Livery*, there a Profert is not
necessary, because it is said the Right claimed depends on something in *Pais*,
to wit, the *Livery*, and therefore the Deed is not full Evidence that the
Conveyance was regularly made; But when a thing lies in *Grant*, there a
Profert is necessary. Things that lie in Livery are those of which Corporeal
Possession may be given; Thing that lie in grant are such of which it cannot
be given, but which must be conveyed by Grant, such as all incorporeal
Hereditaments.—

But I imagine this Distinction is chiefly applicable to the antient Mode
of Conveyance, when Deeds of Feoffment and Livery, since the Introduction
of Uses.—

I suppose all Modern Deeds for the Conveyance [63] of Lands and
Tenements must be accompanied with a Profert, because the uses in the
primitive Idea properly lay in Grant, tho' by the Statute of Uses the Use is
executed and has the same Operation as *Livery of Seisin*. Should your Deed be
Distroyed by Fire or any extraordinary Accident, you must still have a Profert
to Preserve the Form but you will be allowed to prove the Fact, by the best
Evidence the Nature of the Case will admit.—

[64]   PRISONERS & RESCUE

If a Person is taken in Custody by Virtue of any Writ or mesne Process and is Rescued going to Gaol the Sheriff is not liable for he was not Obliged to take the *Posse Commitatus* with him; but the Plaintiff may have an Action on the Case or an Attachment against the Rescuers, and if he Recovers less then his Demand from them he may have an Action against the Original Defendant for the Residue. The Sheriff may in this Case return a Rescue.—

But if the Party be once in Prison either on mesne or final Process and he escapes, the Sheriff is liable; unless by Fresh Pursuit he Retakes the Prisoner before an Action is commenced against him.

So if he is taken on final process and is rescued on his Way to Gaol the Sheriff is liable, for he was bound to take the *Posse Commitatus* with him, and if [65] he did not do it, it was at his own Peril. In all Escapes an action on the Case lies, but in Escapes on final Process the Plaintiff may bring Debt, or Proceed by *Scire facias*, because the Demand is then liquidated and become a Matter of Record; a Writ of Escape may be served on Sunday.—

If a Person is in Custody on mesne Process the Plaintiff must Declare against him in the next ~~said~~ Term to that in which the Writ is Returnable; he must bring the Cause to Trial in two Terms exclusively After Issue Joined, and if he had Obtained a Judgment, he must charge the Prisoner in Execution the first Term to that in which Judgment was signed, or the Prisoner in each Case may by Motion in Court the Term following Obtain a Rule for a Supersedeas.—

In all these Cases it will be proper that [66] the Defendant move for a Supersedeas on Affidavit setting forth that the Plaintiff has neglected to declare against him in two Terms, or to bring on the Trial in three, or to Charge him in Execution in two (as the Case may be) and the Court will make a Rule, upon which the Prisoner files common Bail and sues out a Writ of *Supersedeas* upon which he will be discharged.—

It is a Rule that a Prisoner having been once Superseded, for whatever Cause, can never after be held to special Bail for the same Cause of Action, Although it may have changed its Form, by his giving a Promissory Note &ca—

If he be Superseded for any Omission on mesne Process and the Plaintiff Afterwards takes the necessary Steps and Obtains Judgment, he may again be taken in Execution, but if he has been [67] Superseded in Execution, he cannot be taken on a Second Writ; however I suppose if the Plaintiff should bring an Action of Debt on the Judgment, and Obtain a second Judgment, he may upon that Charge the Defendant in Execution.—

If a Person in Custody is permitted by the Sheriff to go at large, it is an Escape and makes the Sheriff liable. if he is permitted by the Plaintiff to go at Large it is a Release of the Debt & operates as a full Satisfaction & Discharge.—

If a Person is Confined in a House or Gaol, or detained in the Public Streets, or in any other Way suffers a forcible Restraint upon his Liberty, without proper Authority, this amounts to a false Imprisonment, for which he may have an Action, which is commonly coupled with Assault & Battery.—

[68] If he should be Induced under this illegal Restraint to enter into any Contracts, Obligations or Stipulations whatsoever, he may Afterwards avoid them by Pleading *Duress of Imprisonment,* but if he is legally in Custody and enters into any Just & equitable Engagements, he may not Afterwards avoid them on this Pretext.—

It is said in Some Books a Supersedeas does not lie after a Person has been taken in Execution. vide Bacon Title Trespass, Sect false Imprisonment.[61]—

[69]   IMPARLANCE

In England there is an Imparlance of Course, after which the Defendant must plead in Bar, unless in the mean Time he requires a special Imparlance; if he requests a special Imparlance he cannot Afterwards plead in Abatement, unless he saves to himself all manner of Advantages & Exceptions, by doing which he may still plead in Abatement; here there is a Distinction, if he saves to himself all Exceptions only he cannot plead to the Jurisdiction

---

[61] 5 Bacon, *Abridgment* (1768 ed.) 166.

[*Marginal addition:*]

of the Court but he can if he saves to himself

all Advantages as well as Exceptions; the same Rule applies to us it is said, though our Imparlance properly speaking runs until Twenty Days after Term.—

[70] ## NONPROSS & NON SUIT

The Difference between them seems to be this, one takes place before Trial commences the other After Evidence produced by the Plaintiff. In one Case the Meaning seems to be that he does not prosecute or carry on his action: in the other that he does not bring legal Suit, or Sufficient Witnesses, for a non suit takes place for Defect of Evidence.—

[71] ## DEATH

If either of the Parties die pending the Action it abates the Action, but if there are more Plaintiffs than one and one of them dies the Interest or Lien survives, and on Suggestion of the Death of the Party on the Record, the Action may proceed for or against the Survivors.—

Also when there is but one Plaintiff or Defendant and one of them ~~Parties~~ dies After Interlocutory Judgment and before final, a *Scire facias* will lie to have an Inquisition of Damages & Execution for or against the Executors; provided the Action be of such a Kind as could have been Originally brought by or against Executors &c. K B Prac: 409.[63] also Laws of New York.—[64]

Bul nisi prius 306.[62]

---

[62] Buller, *An Introduction to the Law relative to Trials at Nisi Prius* (1st ed. 1772) 306.

[63] 1 Richardson, *The Attorney's Practice in the Court of King's Bench* (4th ed. 1759) 409.

[64] An Act for the better preventing frivolous and vexatious Suits, *5 Col Laws NY* 287 (1772), 288-289.

It is said in some of the Books that if the Party dies after commencing of the Assiz[e] but before Trial it shall not abate the Actio[n] but the Trial may proceed. 2 Bathurst 1415.[65] Raym.[66]

[72] If after Judgment and before Execution sued out, one of the Parties die, regularly by the Books Execution cannot be taken out without a *Sci: fa:* because the Parties are charged.—

If after Execution sued out, it may be Levied without Ceremony; for an Execution say the Books is one intire Thing.—

[73]   MARRIAGE

The Husband by Marriage acquires a Right to all the Goods of the Wife, but nothing more than to the Enjoyment of the Profits of her Land during her Life unless he has a Child by her born alive, after which he has a Just Right to all her Lands, and is stiled Tenant by the Courtesey; the Wife is intitled to one third of all the Husbands Lands after his Death, during her Life, not only those of which he died possessed, but all those of which he was seized at the Time of Marriage or at any Time during Coverture, even tho' aliened in his Life Time, this is called her Dower;[67] nor by the English Law can it be Defeated After Marriage by any other Method then by Levying a Fine in which the Wife must Join After being privately examined as to her voluntary Concurranc[e]

[74] It may be barred before Marriage by a Jointure expressed to be in Lieu of all Dower. By the English Law the Wife can Join her Husband in no Conveyance of her Land, but by fine; but by our Law she may by Deed, after being privately examined by a Judge; It is probable on the same Principle she may release her Dower by joining in a Conveyance of the Husbands Lands.—

If a *Feme sole* is Plaintiff and she marries pending the Action, it may be pleaded in a Plea *puis darein continuance*; but if she is Defendant she cannot take Advantage of her Marriage.—

[65] 2 Bathurst *Introduction to the Law Relative to Trials at Nisi Prius* (1768 ed.) 293.
[66] Burnet v. Holden, T. Raym. 210 (KB 1672).
[67] See Exhibit Q.

If there are several Obligors bound to her as Obligee and she marries one of them, it operates as a Release So I imagine if she Obliges to several Joint Obligees & one of them Marries her, the Relief for the others will be in Equity.[68]

[75] When a Man marries a Woman he makes himself liable for all her Debts while sole, but his responsibility continues only during her Life, for After her Death, whatever may have been not paid or recovered by Judgment in a Suit at Law, he is Released from; Therefore if the Wife dies pending an Action for a Debt due from her while sole, the Lien does not survive but the Action abates, but if Judgment has been given it charges the Husband though Execution has not been sued out. If an Action commence against a Feme sole and she marry and afterwards Judgment be Obtained, she only can be taken in Execution upon a Ca: sa:, but the Husbands goods will be liable (I should suppose)[69] for by Marriage the Husband becomes [76] Proprietor of all the Wifes Goods in Possession with a Right to all her Choses in Action which he Reduces into Possession during her Life; but what has not been Recovered and vested in him, by Judgment of a Court of Law, he cannot after her Death, as Husband recover by Law; but as he is by Law her Administrator he may in that Capacity recover them, subject however to the same Accidents as in the Hands of another Person, that is liable to all her Just Debts; but I imagine all the Residue goes to her Husband.[70] After Marriage all the Debts of the Wife while sole must be sued for against Husband & Wife. When the Cause requires special Bail, the Husband must put in for both; if he does not find Bail, and they are taken in Custody, the Wife on Motion in Court will be liberated [77] on filing common Bail; but if taken on final Process it Appears by some authorities that both will be kept in Custody, but others look a Different way; and I rather believe by the Modern Practice the Wife will be Released.[71]

---

[68] See 1 Coke, *Institutes* *264b.

[69] Wood, *Institutes* (10th ed. 1772) 62.

[70] This conjecture is correct. Administration of the estate of an intestate femme covert went to her husband, and after payment of outstanding debts he would retain the surplus. 5 *Col Laws NY* 618 (1774) (reenacting and modifying 29 Car 2, c. 3, sec. 24 [1678]); Nelson, *Lex Testamentaria* (2d ed. 1728) 59; Wood, *loc. cit. supra* n. 69.

[71] If one is permitted to interpolate to ascertain what the "Modern Practice" was, it appears that Hamilton's belief was a mistaken one. When husband and wife were taken on final process for a debt

If the Husband dies pending the Joint Action, the Lien surviving, the action I imagine survives, but this is too Copious a Subject.—

[78]   DAMAGES

Damages are given on all Torts or Contracts as a Compensation for some Injury done or Right withheld; there are some Actions for the Recovery of Specific Things to which Originally no Damages were Attached; such are all *real Actions, Replevin*[72] *Debt & Detinue.* But there are others which sound Intirely in Damages, and in which the specific Thing is not understood to be claimed but the Value of it; such are all Actions of *Trespass, Trespass on the Case, Trover, Assumpsit,* and all *special Actions; Covenant* may also be Reckoned in this Class.—

But by Statute,[73] in some Real Actions, Damages are given; in Waste for Instance besides the Thing wasted, you Recover treble Damages, this Rather numbered among mixt Actions.—

[79][74]

It is a Rule that the Jury cannot assess more Damages then the Plaintiff claims, for he is supposed best to know what he is intitled to; and therefore if greater Damages happen to be assessed either the Court must order the Excess to be struck off, or the Plaintiff must enter a *Remittitur* for it, and take Judgment for the Ballance, otherwise it would be Error.

---

of the wife incurred while she was single, both would remain in custody. 3 Blackstone, *Commentaries* *414; *NY Laws,* 10 Sess 1787, c. 56, sec. 6; Ex Parte Deacon, 5 Barn. & Ald. 759 (KB 1822). However, if the debt were incurred by the wife during coverture, only the husband would be taken. This latter immunity is described by Blackstone as "one of the greatest privileges of English wives." Blackstone, *id.* This emphasis of the privilege may have led Hamilton to overlook the distinction between debts incurred prior to and during coverture.

[72] For writ of replevin, see Exhibit R.

[73] Statute of Gloucester, 6 Edw 1, c. 5 (1278).

[74] The date "1798" appears at the top of this page in a handwriting different from that of the transcriber. No reason can be advanced for its being there. See n. 14, *supra* at p. 41.

But if the Jury find that the Plaintiff is really intitled to more than he claims, and they wish to give him his due, they may assess Damages to the amount of his Demand, and give Implus in Costs. vide *Bacon* on Damages.—[75]

In joint Trespass if the Parties plead Jointly the Jury must by no means sever the Damages if they should do it, to avoid Error the Plaintiff must make [80] his Election *de melioribus Damnis* and enter a *Nolle Prosequi* for the other. The same Rule (according to Authorities in Bacon Title Damages) applies even when they plead seperately and the Issues are all Tried at the same Time and by the same Jury; but there are Contrary Authorities some say that where the Issues are several and Tried at the same Time, and by the same Jury; as they can at once take into Consideration, the *Quantum* which is a proper Compensation for the Injury, and at the same Time the Propertion of Culpability of each Defendant there they may sever the Damages, and the Plaintiff may have several Executions. vide Carthew.—[76]

Yet these last Authorities may be Questioned on the General Principle of Law, which all Principals in Trespa[ss] [81] and will not allow different Degrees of Guilt in the same Trespass.—

Where seperate Actions are brought, or the Issues on the same Action are Tried at Different Times, several Damages must of Necessity be assessed, but the Plaintiff can only have Execution *de melioribus Damnis* that is his Election among the several Damages of the highest, & Execution for that. He will have *unica taxatio* of Costs for all the Actions.—

[82] **WITNESS**

The Manner of summoning Witness has already been shewn. If a Material Witness be going beyond Sea, the Party whose Witness he is must move the Court for Leave to examine him by Interrogatories; this must be done on Affidavit setting forth, that he is a Material Witness, without whom it would be unsafe to go to Trial; that he is going beyond Sea or out of the

---

[75] 2 Bacon, *Abridgment* (3d ed. 1768) 5.
[76] Rodney v. Strode *et al.*, Carth. 19 (KB 1688).

State and may not Return before the Trial; upon this the Court will make a Rule for him to be examined by Interrogatories before a Judge.—

The Party applying for the Examination must give Notice to the Witness and to the opposite Party to Attend at the Judges Chambers, where he must be sworn & Questioned to wri[tten] Interrogatories.[77] When the Party whose Witness he is has examined him, the Opposite Party must also [83] Examine him to written Interrogatories; his Answers must be put in, in Writing under the Controul & Inspection of the Judge, who will see that his sense and Meaning is Truly expressed without any false Colouring. It has already been said that if the Witness is actually gone out of the State & you wish to put off the Trial, you move the Court on Affidavit, besides stating tha[t] he is a Material Witness &c. you must be particular in Mentioning that he is Expected to Return within a determine[d] Time, not too Remote; for unless there is a prospect, of his returning in a Reasonable Time the Court will not Consent to have the Trial put off; but it is said that if you have Notice of Trial before he leaves the State the Court will not Grant the Delay. If a Witness has been Subpoen[aed] [84] and falls sick on the Way, & you wish the Trial to proceed, you must move the Court on Affidavit specifying the Facts to have him Examined on Interrogatories as in the other Case, and to appoint one of the Judges to be present at the Examination; the Court will appoint one of the Puisne Judges for this Purpose. It will be prudent in the Party to have him sworn before some authorized Person and take a Deposition of the Facts he knows; if he should die in this Situation his Deposition will be admitted as Evidence.—

As to the Sufficiency of a Witness he must be a Person Intirely uninterested, either directly or indirectly, or he cannot be a legal Witness. The Law Carries the Matter of Interest very far; but it would be endless here to enter into all the minute Distinctions that have been made. Commoners are Rejected in Questions relating [85] to the Rights of Common, and Members of a Corporation have been held in Causes where the Corporate Rights were in Dispute, as Insufficient Witnesses. This Matter seems to have been Carried so far as some Times to exclude those Persons who could have been adequate Witnesses in the Matter. It is however a Rule that where the Interest

---

[77] *Compare* interrogatories in Chancery, illustrated at pp. 194-195, *infra*.

is very small or very Remote it shall not destroy the Sufficiency of the Witness; and Lord Hardwick used to say,[78] he never rejected a Witness, but when his Interest was so Great as to occasion a Strong Danger of Perjury; and it is Indeed a wise Rule. Courts have latterally with Reason, been less strict in this Point, and have let any Considerable remote Interest go to the Credit rather than to the Sufficiency of the Witness; however in a late Instance in 3 Burr. *arguendo* the Matter was laid down very strictly.[79]

[86] Also if it be not a vested, but a mere possible or contingent one, it cannot be made an Objection.

When a Witness is introduced and the other side dislikes him he must rise and Inform the Court that he Objects to the Witness, and Assign his Reasons. If the Facts are allowed the Parties may altercate the Law, and the Judges Determine, but if the Facts are disputed, the Court will hear Witnesses to establish or refute them. It is common when the Witness is only suspected and no Facts are alledged, to have him sworn upon his *voir dire,*

[*Marginal addition:*]

a very improper Method to ascertain the Interest of a Witness—because if he is so much interested in the Event of the suit as to be biased in his testimony there is a strong presumption that he will not suffer himself [to be] precluded from testifying[80]

that is, he is sworn to answer truly such Questions as shall be put to him respecting any Interest he may have in the Cause depending; the Judges then ask him if he has any Interest, direct or consequently in, or if he will gain or lose anything by the Event of the Suit, & [87] according to his Answer he is rejected or admitted. No Relation other then Husband & Wife disqualifies a Witness, Altho other Relations may effect their credibility. Yet what the Wife has been heard to say on another Occasion may be Evidence against the Husband.—

----

[78] Rex v. Bray, Cas. T. Hard. 358 (1737).

[79] Apparently Rex v. Haydon, 3 Burr. 1387 (1763 KB).

[80] Apparently inserted by person "A." See n. 36, *supra*. Through use and age, the last portion of this insert has become indecipherable.

When Subpoena Tickets are served you must tender Expences, those are one Shilling when the Witness lives in the County where the Cause is to be Tried and four Shillings & six pence if he lives in another County.

In the Cause of Lord Audley for a Rape his Wife was Admitted as a Witness against him, State Trials page 122.—[81]

[88]   JUDGMENT & EXECUTION

By the common Law Judgment related to the first Day of the Term of which it was given and bound the Lands of the Defendant from that Time; and it does so still except as to *bona fide* Purchasers. But now by the Statute it only binds the Lands, as to these from the Time of actually ~~signing~~ filing & docketting the same. By the common Law also the Goods were bound from the Teste of the Writ of Execution, and it continues the same, except with Respect to *bona fide* Purchasers, as to them it only binds from the Actual Delivery of the Writ to the Sheriff.—[82]

If Execution is not taken out in a Year After Judgment, it cannot be done Afterwards without reviving the Judgment by *Scire facias.* but if Execution hath once been Issued out, it may be Continued on [89] Roll by *vice comes non misit Breve,* till the Time of Serving it.—

Any Time within ten Years Judgment may be revived by *Sci: fa:* of Course, but after ten years you must move the Court for Leave to sue it out, and your Motion must be founded on Affidavit setting forth that the Parties are living, and that the Judgment or Part of it is yet unsatisfied; this is the same whether a Writ of Execution has in the mean Time been sued out or not. This last Clause is not Law, vide K B Prac. 402.—[83]

----

[81] 3 Howell, *State Trials* 414 (1631). For convenience and to avoid confusion we have converted the citation to the volume and page of Howell's *State Trials,* the latest edition of *State Trials.* Cf. also *infra* n. 72, at p. 797.

[82] An Act for Prevention of Frauds and Perjuryes, 29 Car 2, c. 3, sec. 14, 15 (1678); 2 Bacon, *Abridgment* (3d ed. 1768) 363.

[83] K B Prac. [1 Richardson, *The Attorney's Practice in the Court of King's Bench* (4th ed. 1759)] 402 contradicts the preceding statement. It is probable that either Hamilton made this correction to whatever source he had been consulting for "Judgment and Execution," or that the person transcribing our copy of *Practical Proceedings* made this correction as an interpolation to Hamilton's work. The correcting sentence is in the same hand in which the rest of the volume is transcribed.

There are two Writs of Execution in Use & with us, Altho our Statutes speak of a third, the *Elegit;*[84] these in Use are the *Ca: sa:*[85] which operates upon the Person, & the *fi: fa:*[86] which operates upon the Land & Tenements, Goods & Chattels. The English *Fi: fa:* affected [90] only Chattels ours the Real Estate equally; this Extension of it was by Act of Parliament of Geo: 2d. particularly made for this Country, a memorable Statute & which Admitted more then our Legislature ought to have assented to; it was one of the Highest Acts of Legislature that one Country could exercise over another.—[87]

In Executing the Writ of *Ca: sa:*, if the Sheriff once touch the Defendant he may justify breaking open Houses to take him. But if an outer Door be open, he can Justify breaking open an Inner Door, in Executing the Writ of *Fi: fa:*; also he may open inner, but not outer Doors, he may break open a Barn or any other but the Dwelling House, or an out House annexed to it, to get at the goods of the Defendant. If a Question [91] should be made about the Property of the Goods, he may take Notice of it at his Peril, and must summon a Jury to Inquire into the Property, and if they Determine it to be in the

---

[84] The writ of *elegit* was first given by the statute Westminster 2, 13 Edw 1, c. 18 (1285). Prior to this the common law, influenced by feudal restrictions against alienation of lands, permitted satisfaction of a judgment from chattels and present profits of lands only. With the *elegit*, if the appraised value of the defendant's chattels did not satisfy the debt, one-half of the lands held in his name or in trust for him were delivered to the plaintiff, who became tenant by *elegit* until out of the rents and profits of the lands the judgment was satisfied, or until the defendant's interest in the lands expired. Blackstone states that this taking of actual possession of a defendant's lands was considered to be an extreme measure "of so high a nature" that in most situations, after the issue of an *elegit*, the defendant's body was no longer liable to a *capias ad satisfaciendum*. 3 Blackstone, *Commentaries* 418, 419. For the form of the elegit, see Exhibit S.

[85] See Exhibit T.

[86] See Exhibit U.

[87] The statute to which Hamilton refers is 5 Geo 2, c. 7, sec. 4 (1732). Just as Englishmen considered the *elegit* to be an extreme measure, New York colonists resented the extension of the application of the writ of *fieri facias*, normally effective only to gain execution of goods and chattels, to permit execution against real property interests. The preamble of the statute indicates that it was enacted for the benefit of British creditors. Hamilton's observation that this statute ought not to have been assented to by the colonial legislature reflects pre-Revolutionary thinking that Acts of Parliament unrelated to the traditional corpus of Navigation Acts were unconstitutional because the Colonies were not represented in Parliament. Since Hamilton had participated in the pamphlet war, he could hardly fail to be aware of the fact that not only did Parliament's legislative jurisdiction extend to the Colony, but colonial enactments could be disallowed by the King in Council. Assent of the Colonial Assembly was not required in order that parliamentary enactments be effective in the Colony. Another example of Hamilton's unorthodox views respecting colonial legislation (or perhaps his lack of information) can be seen on pp. [133]-[134] of his manuscript and in the editor's footnote there cited.

Defendant, the Sheriff is safe in going on, whether the Determination be well founded or not.—

The Sheriff may break the House of a Stranger after leave Demanded, & Refusal, If he has good Information the Goods of the Defendant are concealed there.—

If the Defendant is taken on a *Ca: sa:* & escapes or dies in Prison, the Plaintiff may Afterwards have Execution against his Property if he has any. In Case of Death, Fi: fa: shall not Extend to goods sold *bona fide* after Judgments, to pay Creditors.—

If *Fi: fa:* is sued out and Part is levied of the Goods, he may have an alias or Pluries [92] till the Demand is satisfied; but the Fi: fa: must be specially Returned, that the Sheriff has Caused to be made, so much, Part of the Debt and Damages (or *Damages* only as the case may be) and that there were no Goods of which he could cause to be made, the Residue. If it should be Returned generally, whatever might be the Fact as to the satisfaction, no other could be sued out.—

The first Writ of Execution must always follow the Judgment, and issue in the same County where the Venue is laid; if the Defendant lives in another County or his Property there, there must be a *Testatum Ca: sa:*[88] or *Fi: fa:*; also if a Part of the Debt or Damages be Levied in one County and the Defendant has Property in another, a *Testatum* must Issue in that County. but is not necessary [93] in the first Instance, that a Writ should be Issued out, the *Testatum* will suffice, & Supposition will be taken for Fact.

If the Execution has been suspended by a Writ of Error beyond the year, it may on Affirmance of the Judgement, be sued out without a Sci: fa:. If it has been stayed by an Injunction from Chancery, the Authorities differ, some say it may afterwards be sued out without a Sci: fa: and others say the Courts of Law will not take Notice of Chancery Proceedings, and it need not have prevented suing out Execution, although it would not have carried into Effect.

If the Party has Confessed Judgment with a *cessat Executio* entered on the Roll, no *Sci: fa:* will be necessary, and the Court will Oblige the Party to Confirm to the Record, and will [94] compel him to make Restitution, if Contrary thereto he takes out Execution, before the *Cassat* is expired; but if

---

88 See Exhibit V.

there be an agreement for a Stay of Execution extraneous to the Record, the Court will take no Notice of it.—

The *Habere facias possessionem*[89] is an Executory Writ used in Ejectment to restore the Plaintiff to the Possession of the Thing recovered; this is Returnable in Fact at the Election of the Plaintiff, to secure to him an indisputable Possession; for if the Writ be once returned, and the Plaintiff should be ousted by the Person from Whom he recovered possession, he would be driven to a second Action; but if the Writ is not Returned he may be put in Possession again by another Writ, and the first will be entered on the Record by *Vice comes non misit Breve*.

[95] If a Person has Judgment against two jointly bound, he ought to levy the Debt in equal Proportions upon the Property of both, otherwise the Party on whom the whole is levied may have Relief by an *Audita querela*, yet if he levies Part on one, and Afterwards can find nothing belonging to the other, he cannot resort to the first.—

If the Goods of a Tenant be taken in Execution the landlord may distrain for one years Rent in the Sheriffs Hands, but if he gives Notice to the Sheriff of his Demand, the Sheriff is bound to retain it for him.—

[96]   COSTS[90]

Costs were not originally given to either Party, they were first allowed by the Stat. of Gloucester to Plaintiffs,[91] Afterwards to Defendant, who are now entitled to them in most Actions.—

It is a Rule that in Actions in which Damages before that Statute of Gloucester were given, when they have been doubled or trebled by Statute, Costs, are doubled & trebled also.—But in Actions where the Damages are intirely created by Statute, and they are doubled or trebled, only singal Costs are allowed.—

---

[89] See Exhibit W.
[90] See Exhibit X.
[91] Statute of Gloucester, 6 Edw 1, c. 1 (1278).

In Actions against Officers, relative to the Execution of their Office, when Judgment is in their Favor they are entitled to Costs. Executors who bring in Actions in the Right of their Testator, where the Cause arose in his Life time [97] are not liable to Costs; but where the Cause of Action arose Afterwards, and is of a Nature that the Action might as well have been commenced in the Name of the Executor[92] himself, he is then liable to Costs; so he is at all Times if he suffers himself to be nonprossed, but not when he is nonsuited; (for this Distinction vide 3 Burrows)[93] and at all Times when he is Defendant he is Subject to Costs.—

The same Rule applies to Administrators, and perhaps to Heirs *sed quere*.—[94]

Costs are allowed on a Sci: fa: if the Party appear & plead; but not otherwise.—[95]

Neither Plaintiff or Defendant recover Costs in Abatement, decided on Demurrer.—

[98] There is a Statute that says, that where in Trespass of several kinds the Damages do not exceed forty Shillings, the Plaintiff shall have no more

---

[92] Original Ms. reads *Execution,* which has been corrected, in different ink and handwriting, to *Executor.*

[93] Hawes, Exec v. Saunders, 3 Burr. 1584 (KB 1764).

[94] Payment of costs was at the court's discretion. If an executor brought suit for a claim which had arisen while the decedent was alive, but the action was nonsuited, usually the executor would be permitted to escape personal liability for costs. This was on the rationale that since he was bringing an action in another's right he could not have been well informed about the cause of action and therefore should not be held liable for costs incurred through no fault of his. The opposite result would occur if some fault, delay, or vexation in bringing the suit were his. Hawes, Exec v. Saunders, 3 Burr. 1584 (KB 1764); Bennet, Admr v. Coker, 4 Burr. 1927-1929 (1767).

An executor or administrator, according to Hamilton, would be fully liable for costs on an action brought by him which had accrued after the death of the decedent. An application to exempt an heir from paying costs on suits brought in behalf of the estate which had arisen during the decedent's lifetime would not be made for a suit brought by an heir, and Hamilton's quaere is well taken, although his supposition is not. Only executors named in the will, or administrators duly appointed, had a right to bring suit in behalf of the deceased and thereby be exempt from costs. No one else could bring such an action, and anyone assuming this authority without claim to the office of executor or administrator would be an executor *de son tort.* Implicit in Hamilton's supposition that an heir might be exempt from costs was his incorrect assumption that an heir could bring such a suit. Either Hamilton was poorly informed about who had the power to bring suit in behalf of an estate, or he did not recognize the implications of his statement concerning costs. In any event, he did not make full use of the information which he almost certainly had at hand, for in Jacob's *Law Dictionary* (7th ed. 1756), under the title *Executor de Son Tort,* it is explicitly stated that only an *authorized* executor or administrator can bring suit for the estate.

[95] See n. 118, *infra.*

Costs than Damages, unless the Judge shall certify, that a Right of Freehold came in Question or that the Trespass was of a Wilful malicious Kind.[96] Now by Statute where there are two Defendants in an Action of Trespass, and one acquitted the other found guilty, the one acquitted shall be entitled to Costs, unless the Judge before whom the Cause is Tried will certify, that there was probable Ground to make him Defendant.—[97]

[99]   SCIRE FACIAS[98]

This is a Judicial Writ, in Nature of an Action, which Issues for a Variety of Purposes in the Law, commanding the Sheriff to make known to the Party, to appear and shew, if any thing he knows or has to say for himself, why a Particular Thing should not be done. It issues to revoke a grant of the Sovereign when it has been made on false suggestions, or erroneous Grounds.—

It issues as has before been seen to revive a Judgment when Execution has not been taken out within a Year and a Day; and in this Case it must follow the Judgment, that is, it must Issue in the same County where the Venue is laid. It issues in all Cases where there has been Judgment against a Person which cannot be executed upon him, to Charge those who are not Parties, but Privies to the Judgment, or who are by any other Means bound to satisfy, as against *the Bail,* [100] for their Principal against, *Heirs, Tenants, Executors, Administrators,* for the deceased.—

Against Executors, and it must follow the Judgment. Against Bail it may either issue in the County where the Action was brought, or in that where the Bail was put in before Commissioners in the County. When you want to sue out a Sci: fa: against Bail, you must first make out a Recognizance Roll, this must be Capped of the Term the Declaration is of, it must have the Memorandum as on Issue Rolls with the Declaration, then follows the Coming in of the Bail, and their becoming Manucaptors and pledges &c.—

---

[96] 22 & 23 Car 2, c. 9 (1672-1673).
[97] An Act for the better preventing frivolous and vexatious Suits, 5 *Col Laws NY* 287 (1772).
[98] See Exhibit Y.

and here it ends.—It must be left in the office when you get the Sci: fa: sealed. The same is made out when you [101] bring an Action of Debt on the Recognizance, this proceeding seems to be without use, nor do the Books explain its Intention, but it seems it is still followed. When you wish to give Actual Warning this is done on the first Sci: fa: and the Sheriff Returns a *Sci: feci:* purporting that by honest and Lawful men of his Bailwic he has caused to be made known to the Parties concerned that they are to be before the People &c. on the Time prescribed in the Writ If no warning is given he returns, "Nihil habuit," that is, that the Parties have nothing in his Bailwic by which he can make known Neither are they found in the same; then there Issues a second Sci: fa: tested the Day of the Return of the first, and the Sheriff makes the same Return two Nihils it is said amount to a *Scire feci* & [102] have in many Respects the same Incidents.—

When the *Sci: feci:*, or the last Nihil is Returned the Plaintiff gives a Rule that the Defendant plead in Twenty Days or Judgment; if he appears & pleads Issue is joined, And the Action proceeds as in a common Case, liable to the same Rules Hence it Appears, that the Sci: fa: is in Nature of a Declaration.—

There is a compound Writ called a *Scire fieri inquiry*, which is used when an Executor or Administrator suffers Judgment to go against him by Default.—**99**

There is a special Ca: sa: or Fi: fa: on Judgment after a Sci: fa:; after as appears to us of Record "you Insert this Clause" Wherefore in our Court before us [103] it was considered that the said A ought to have his Execution against the said B of the Debt and Damages aforesaid.—

A Sci: fa: as well as an Action of Debt or assumpsit lies against a Sheriff when upon any final process he suffers an Escape, or Rescue of goods, or when having levied the Money he withholds, but in this Case an Attachment will also lie; If the Defendant appears and pleads to the Sci: fa:, in your *Venire, Distringes* & *Jurata,* After the words "in a Plea of &c: (as the Case may be) you must Insert whereupon a Scire facias &c:"—

You cannot plead in Abatement of a Sci: fa: what you might have pleaded in the Original Action.—

---

99 See n. 118, *infra.*

Scire facias is not amendable but if bad must be quashed.—1 Stra. 401.—[100]

[104]   ISSUES & JUDGMENT ROLLS

When Issue is joined you make up your Issue Roll which must be Capped of the Term Issue is joined, then follow the Warrants of Attorney, then the Memorandum, then the Declaration, the Plea, Replication &ca. to the Joining of Issue; and if the Action is not brought on the[101] to[101] Trial the same Term, the Venire must be Continued on the Roll till the Term in which the Cause is Tried by *Vice comes non misit breve.*—

There are four Distinctions in the Form of the Memorandum; when Issue is joined in the same Term with the Declaration; when it is joined of another Term; when it is more then four Terms After; when the Cause of Action Arises in the same Term of [105] which Declaration is, in which Case the Declaration is of a Particular Day in Term

In General, at whatever Time the Declaration is delivered, it by Fiction of Law relates to the first Day of the Term, and in the Records it is entered accordingly, but in the last Case above mentioned it is necessary to depart from the Rule and not deprive the Plaintiff of his Remedy or procrastinate it by such a Fictious Relation.—

If the Cause is tried at Bar the Issue Roll must be brought into Court on the Day of Trial & delivered to the Judges.—

If at *Nisi prius* it must be filed in the Office when you carry your *Nisi prius* Records to be sealed you make up your *Nisi prius* Records thus.

After the Caption, you make a Transcript of the Issue Roll to the awarding [106] the first Venire inclusively, and then at a little distance below you begin with a New Caption; then follows the Jurata, the award of the *Distringas,* & the *Suendum*[102] [*Sciendum*], which Concluds the Record. The sec-

---

[100] Hillier v. Frost, 1 Str. 404 (KB 1721).

[101] The underlining of "the" may indicate that the marginal note "to" (in different handwriting) was meant as a replacement, changing the phrase to "brought on to trial."

[102] Error in Ms.

ond *Placita,* supplies the Place of Continuances When you have made out your *Nisi prius* Record you carry it together with the Issue Roll to the Office, you file the Issue Roll there and get the Nisi prius Record sealed, which is done by winding a bit of Tape round the Roll & sealing the End.—

After having sued out your Venire with a *Nisi prius Clause,* Subpoenaed your Witnesses &c. at the Time Appointed you carry down your Record to the ~~Assizes~~ Sittings[103] and Inform the Court, that you have a Record in a Cause between [107] AB & CD, which you pray may be Read & filed; you then Deliver it to the Clerk who reads it accordingly; this is done the first Day of the ~~Assizes~~ Sittings.—[104]

When your Cause is Tryed the history of the Proceedings is indorsed on the nisi prius Record, which is called a *Postea* and Carried up the Beginning of the next Term to the Court above in the Manner we have already seen. In common Cases the Clerk of Nisi prius, whose proper Business it is, makes up the *Postea,* but when there is any special Verdict, which may Require greater Skill & Care, the Attorney will prefer making them up himself.—

The next Step is to make up the Record or Judgment Roll, this is a Continuation of the Issue Roll by a *Postea inde processa continuatio,* afterwards [108] the Process being Continued Between the Parties aforesaid &Ca., then follow the Postea, and then the Judgment of the Court, therefore it is Considered &Ca. The Proceedings afterwards have already been mentioned.—

It is said in *Gilbert,*[105] that the Inde *Processa Continuatio* makes the Continuances before mentioned on the Issue Roll un[ne]cessary.—

Note, With us we do not make up the *Distringas,* tho' it is pretended by some it is proper in Juries of View, but the Reasons assigned are not satisfactory, and the Practice will Justify the dispensing with the Distringas in this Case as well as in others.[106] As was before Observed should the Venire be returned & the Trial postponed, in summoning the Jury anew you may use a Distringas, but I believe another Venire might do.—[107]

---

[103] The word *Sittings* is apparently a correction by person "A." See n. 36, *supra.*

[104] See n. 103, *supra.*

[105] Gilbert, *History and Practice of the Court of Common Pleas* (1737) 79-81.

[106] See *supra,* p. [10], and n. 6, pp. 67-68.

[107] *Ibid.*

[109]   HABEAS CORPUS[108]

This Writ is made use of for the Purpose of Removing Prisoners from one Court to another, for the more easy Administration of Justice, this seems to be its principal Use, tho' it may be to remove a Prisoner from one Place to another ad testificandum &c. The first is the *Habeas Corpus cum causa ad faciandum et recipiandum*, it is made out by an Atty of the Party applying for it, directed to the Judges of the Inferior Court with their proper stile and Title commanding them to have the Body of the Party under sure & safe Conduct before the Court on a certain Day, together With the Day & Cause of his Caption & Detention to do & Receive all those things which then & there shall be Considered of him.—

In England this Writ is commonly made returnable before a Judge, but as the [110] Reasons do not apply here, it is best to make it Returnable at once before the Court.—

When you have made out a Habeas Corpus you carry it to a Judge who writes upon it, Allowed this ____ Day of ____ 1787   R. M. Chief Justice you then carry it to the Office and get it sealed   you then carry it to the Court below at their next Session, informing the Court, that you have a Habeas Corpus in such a Cause, you pray that it may be read and filed, you then deliver it to the Clerk who reads it, and the Court then become possessed of it and are bound to proceed accordingly.—

It is the Business of the Court to send up the Return, which they do by delivering it to the Person in whose favor it was granted; the Form of the Return is this "The Execution of the within Writ [111] Appears by the Schedule annexed" This the Court Indorse on the back of the Writ, the schedule annexed is Directed to the Chief Justice of the Supreme Court, Certifying agreeable to the Requisition of the Writ, the Cause and Day of the Caption and Detention.

The Defendant then carries up the Return at the proper Time to the Superior Court, inform the Court that he has Such a Return, and prays that it may be read and Filed; it Is then properly before the Court.—

[108] See Exhibit Z.

In all Cases of Habeas Corpus, special Bail must be put in, except for words and small Trespasses; in this Country it must be put in, in all Cases except Persons suing in *autre droit* as Executors &c. Instead of a *Cepi Corpus*, the Bail Piece specifies, *Habeas Corpus*, and instead of the Plaintiffs Name says at the [112] suit of the Plaintiff in the Plaint.

If the Plaintiff in the Original Action chuses to proceed in the Court above he must at the Return of the Writ move for a Rule that the Defendant put in Bail to the Action in 20 Days or a *Procendando*.[109] And A Cause once remanded by a *Procedendo*, cannot again be removed by a Habeas Corpus; If the Bail in the Inferior Court become Bail above, the Plaintiff cannot object. The Plaintiff hath 28 Days to Except to Bail on a Habeas Corpus.—

If the Plaintiff does not move for a Rule & deliver a Declaration in the second Term after the Writ is Returned, the Deft. is not bound to Except it afterwards, but he cannot in this Case nonpross the Plaintiff or Oblige him to pay Costs, for he is not supposed to be in Court; but if he has appeared and Paid the Defendant [113] under a Rule, and Neglects to declare in Time, he may be nonprossed, & Subject to Costs; if the Cause is Remanded by a *Procedendo* the Defendant pays Costs.—

There seems to be no Mode pointed out for the Recovery of Costs of Removal, in Case the Cause be afterwards sent Down to the Court below by a procedendo; but I suppose the taxed Bill of Costs will be sent down with it.—[110]

The Record is never removed by a Habeas Corpus delivered after the one of the Jurors sworn, which[111] comes too late; a[112] Habeas Corpus shall not be Received by a Court of Record having Jurisdiction to hold Pleas in the Cause, unless delivered before Issue & Demurrer joined if Issue or Demurrer is not joined within six Weeks after Arrest or appearance it is said that the Plaintiff when he Declares may after[113] his Cause   alter[113] of Action from what it was in the Court below: sed quere.—

---

[109] See Exhibit AA.

[110] Costs would be taxed. RM 1654 sec. 22; KBRM 1654 sec. 25 CP.

[111] The word *which* is apparently inserted by person "A." See n. 36, *supra*.

[112] See n. 111, *supra*.

[113] Inserted in margin to correct "after" in text. Apparently made by person "A." See n. 36, *supra*.

[114]   CERTIORARI[114]

You obtain a Certiorari in the same Manner as you do a *Habeas Corpus* and you carry it Down in the same Manner; it is usual for the winning Party to make up the Record for the Court below carry it to the Court above pray that it may be Read & filed, and made a *Consilium*, a Day is appointed to give Judgment, and in the meantime the Parties exhaust themselves in Argument, the Party that sues out the *Certiorari* first giving the Court a State of the Exceptions.—

If the Justice or Justices do not return the Certiorari, according to the Requisition of the Writ the Term following, the Party that sued it out may lay him or them under a Rule to make Return to the same by the first Day of the next Term, or shew Cause why an Attachment should not issue. This Rule must be served on the Justice or Justices.—

A *Certiorari* Issues to an Inferior Court to remove the Record generally, After Judgment in the Court below.—[115]

[115]   CORPORATIONS

Your first Process is a Summons, if they do not appear by Attorney you take your distress infinite, this being an Artificial Body there can be no Attachment or Arrest.—

---

[114] See Exhibit BB.

[115] The statement requires explanation. From an inferior Court of Common Pleas writs of error would lie. The use of certiorari to review was confined in England to causes which did not proceed according to the course of the common law, viz., where no jury lay. (Groenvelt v. Burwell, 1 Salk 263 [KB 1698].) The records show that certiorari was so used in colonial New York to review such determinations as orders in bastardy and orders for the settlement of paupers. Since justices of the peace in New York were given a petty civil jurisdiction, with jury optional on payment for it, both error and certiorari were used. In 1765 an Act of Assembly was passed to restrain these reviews. 4 *Col Laws NY* 861. So far as review from Common Pleas Courts was concerned, an act of 1769 sought to limit such to writs of attaint and error but this was disallowed. 4 *Col Laws NY* 1088. A state statute which empowered justices of the peace to try causes up to £10 contemplated either writ of error or certiorari for review. *NY Laws,* 5 Sess 1782, c. 36.

[116]   JOINT PARTNERS

When two are jointly bound and one cannot be found on the Process, in England, you must proceed against him by outlawry till you compel an Appearance, before you ~~could~~ can go on against the other who did appear; but with us the Legislature have prescribed another Remedy, authorising you to proceed against both as if they were both taken, to Judgment, and to take out Execution against both, but you are not permitted to levy Execution either on the Person, or sole property of him who did not appear. When one of them lives in one County and the other in another, take out a Writ, with a *respondendum simul cum* Clause in it, and then proceed on the above Act passed 19th. Feby. 1756.[116] You may bring them in by taking out similar Writs Running into each County. If you [117] bring an Action of Assumpsit against two, and both appear, one employs an Atty and pleads *non Assumpsit*, the other does not, and makes Default; you must take out a *Venire* to summon a Jury *tam ad inquirandum quam ad triandum*, you will enter Judgment by Default against one, and the Jury will Assess intire Damages if you have a Verdict against the other.—

Joint Tenants of Lands or Goods regularly must sue and declare jointly, if they be wronged thereon; But Tenants in Common tho' they are to join in personal Actions yet in Real, and Assize and Slander of Title they ought to sever. The Rule in personal Actions is, that one may Join several Torts & Wrongs in the same Declaration & Writ, so they be of one Nature and against the same Person.—

If one Trespass be done by divers persons [118] The Plaintiff may make it either Joint or several as he pleases, and yet two that Join in a Trespass do so make one Trespasser that one is Answerable for the other, and if they are sued in one Action they may sever in Pleas & Issues, and a Release to one is a Release to all: also the Jury must assess Damages for all on each, but there shall be but one Satisfaction.

When a Joint Action lies against several and some of their Names are known and some not, the Action may be brought against such as are known, by their Particular Names, and declare with a *Simul cum alias*.

---

[116] An Act to Enable Creditors to Recover their Debts more easily from joint-partners, 4 *Col Laws NY* 18 (1756).

[119]   JOINT ACTIONS

You may comprise several Actions in the same Declaration but they must agree in Nature; Actions founded on Torts must go together, and those Contracts, also *Debt* & *Detinue*, *Trespass* and a special Action of *Trespass on the Case*, may be joined; but not Debt and Trespass; Trover & Assumpsit cannot be joined, because they are founded on Different Foundations.—There is the usual Confusion in this Doctrine.—

You cannot have more then four Defendants for Different Cause of Action in one Writ, nor more then four Witnesses in one Subpoena.—

It is laid down in *Bacon*[117] that two Actions f[o]unded on Substantia[l] Injuries, or in other Words two principal Actions cannot be Joined; as Trespass & Trover, tho' both founded on *Tort* cannot be joined; but as was said above, Trespass and any special [120] Action on the Case may, for the latter is Considered as an auxilary Action & brought in Aggravation of Damages, rather than as a principal Cause itself; but all the Books say *Debt* & *Detinue* two principal Actions.—

The Reason why you cannot join Actions founded on the *Tort* with those founded on the *Contract* is said to be, because the Judgment is different, one is the *Capiatur pro fine* and the other *in Miserecordia*, in Mercy; where two Defendants confess Trespass, the Damages are not severed.—

[121]   INFANTS

Infants may sue either by *Prochein ami* or *Guardian*, but they must always Defend by Guardian. The regular Method for obtaining leave to sue is by the Infants petitioning the Court, the next Friend or Guardian signifies his Willingness to undertake it, and A third Person as Witness makes Oath that the Petition & Certificate were duly signed It would seem however that the Court or Judge in Vacation might admit this formality the Allowance is made in Form of a Bail Piece and signed by the Judge. If the Infant will not appear

---

[117] 1 Bacon, *Abridgment* (3d ed. 1768) 30.

by Guardian in a suit against him, the Plaintiff may move the Court to appoint one for him—Unless the Plaintiff procures the Admission to sue by Guardian the Defendant is not bound to answer.

[122] An Ideot cannot sue or Defend otherwise than in Person—A Lunatic if underage by Guardians, if of full Age by Attorney.—

In suit for an Infant there are no Pledges of prosecution, and the Guardians Name is signed under instead of the Attorneys.—

EXECUTORS

Although an Executors Power & Right only relates to Personallities, he may bring an Ejectment because that goes for Damages as well as Possession of the Lands, also it may be for a Term of Years.—

Your Action against Executors may be brought against all or against those [123] that act only, for you are not bound to know them but by their administering.—

Executors cannot be held to Bail as Such until a Devastavit returned. If you obtain Judgment against an Executor it is doubtful by the Books whether you can have Execution *de bonis propriis*, till after a Return *Nulla Bona* to a Writ against the *Bona Testatoris* and a *Sci: fa:* to shew Cause.—

But some of our Practitioners hold you may at once take out Execution *de bonis Testatoris si non* then *de bonis Propriis*.—This you can clearly do as to Costs, but I doubt it as to *Principal Debt* & Damages.—**118**

---

118 Both methods of securing execution of an executor's property were used. Wyche states that the preferred method (because with it the defendant had to appear and plead, and so costs could be assessed against him) was first to have a *fieri facias* returned *nulla bona,* then to issue a *scire fieri* inquiry for the sheriff to see if the executor had committed waste, and finally to issue a *scire facias* for the defendant to show cause why his goods should not be taken in execution. Wyche, *NY Supreme Court Practice* (2d ed. 1794) 222. For a discussion of this procedure in English law, and the manner in which King's Bench and Common Pleas practices were combined in the *scire fieri* inquiry, see 1 Will. Saund. 219 n. 2.

[124]   REFERRENCE

The Doctrine of Referrence with us is founded upon an Act of our Legislature[119] which authorizes the Court in Cases of complex Accounts which are Improper for Consideration of Juries, with or without Consent of Parties to appoint Persons to examine & determine; if the Parties consent, they may agree on the Referrees or may chuse to have them appointed by the Court.—

There are three Referrees; if either Party wish to have the Matter referred, he may move the Court, and on shewing probable Cause for his Motion it will be granted; if this is not done by either Party, the Court is Authorized from the Face of the Proceedings to do it from their own Pleasure; for this purpose they wait until Issue produced which enables [125] them to Judge of the Nature of the Case. In either Case they make a Rule ordering the Matter to be Referred to Referrees named in the Rule & Requiring them to examine the Allegations of the Parties & Report Accordingly.—

The Party Applying for the Rule or the Plaintiff when the Referrence Originates with the Court, serves a Certified Copy of it upon each Referree, who have a Meeting according to the Exigency of the Rule, and appoint a Day in Writing for the Examination; the Party Applying indorses this Appointment on another Copy of the Rule and serves it upon the opposite Party. Both Parties then take out Subpoenas for their Witnesses & serve them as in other Cases; the Subpoena however is special, reciting Referrence Particularly. On the Day Appointed the Parties attend [126] With their Witnesses & a Magistrate is provided by the Party Applying to swear the Referrees according to the Act, and also the Witnesses.—

The Matter afterwards proceeds as on an Inquiry, and when finished the Referrees make their Report & deliver it in Writing to the prevailing Party,— who carries it up to Court, and on the Day appointed, or if none has been appointed, on the first Day of the Subsequent Term holding the Report in his hand and briefly informing the Court what it is he prays that it may be read

---

[119] An Act for the better Determination of personal Actions, depending upon Accounts, *NY Laws*, 4th Sess 1781, c. 25, sec. 2.

& filed after it has been read by the Cerk he prays that the Report may stand confirmed & Judgment *Nisi causa.*—

I take it for Granted he gives the usual Notice of his Intended motion to the opposite Party and a Copy of the Report.—

[127] The Rule *nisi Causa* is a Rule of Course & Notice must be taken of it by the opposite Party without Service, it is as usual, a four Days Rule if the Report is for Plaintiff in the Cause he enters Judgment with a *Relicta verificatione* and a *Cognovit Actionem*; if for the Defendant he enters Judgment in the Form of a Nonpross.—

That is when Pltff is Exr.
Vide Stat. 2d. Vol
103.[120]

If the Report finds that there is a Ballance in Favour of the Defendant, it stands as a Debt of Record for which he may have a Sci: fa:.

The Referrees are allowed eight Shillings a Day besides Reasonable Expences in the first Instance by the Winning Party and allowed in Costs on the Judgment. There is also a Refference at Common Law by Consent of the Parties I suppose our Proceedings in this Case resemble those in the foregoing except that the Rule is more Particular, and supplies the Place of Law.—[121]

[128]   AC-ETIAMS

In all Cases not bailable of Course which are of Sufficient Importance to Require Bail, the Plaintiff must make Affidavit of the Nature of the Case and apply to the Judge to order it. The Judge if he think proper to allow Bail indorses upon the Back of the Affidavit, "Let Bill of Albany (or New York as the Case may be, or Capias) Issue against AB with an Ac-etiam of £20 at the suit of CD. Upon this Affidavit Dated &c. R. M."—

If the Judges order for an Ac-etiam be not well founded; the Defendant has a Right to Apply to the Court or Judge to be discharged, who may direct

---

[120] 2 *Laws of NY* (Greenleaf ed. 1792) 103. This marginal comment to *Practical Proceedings* is in a different hand and must have been inserted after 1792.

[121] The reference by consent had a statutory basis. An Act for determining Differences by Arbitration, 9 Will 3, c. 15 (1697-1698).

according to circumstances.—But I doubt whether there is any Application to a Judge,[122] I imagine the Plaintiff puts his Ac-etiam of Course and lets the Defendant have his Remedy, by laying him under a [129] Rule to shew Cause of Action.

In your Ac-etiam in this Court it is the common practice to make double that sum.

By Statute 13 Car 2.[123] you cannot hold the Deft. to special Bail without expressing the Cause of Action in the Writ; this has given rise to the *Ac-etiam Billa* which are inserted in Writs, after commanding the Sheriff to take the Defendant and haveing him before the Court to answer the Plaintiff of a Plea of Trespass, you add "And also to a Bill of the said A against the said B for one hundred pounds of Debt (or upon promise &c. as the Case may be) according to the Custom of our Court before us to be Exhibited &c:"[124] If in Covenant you say, "for a Breach of Covenant to the Damage of the said A of £100 &c:" If in Trespass, "For taking and carrying away the Goods of the said A, to his Damage of £100." If in Assumpsit, "For [130] nonperformance of Certain Promises and undertakings to the Damage of the said A. of £100 or more commonly for £100 upon Promise.—If in Trover, "for Converting & disposing of the Goods and Chattles of the said A to the Value of £100. In Debt, on Recognizance against Bail there is also an *Ac-etiam Clause*, but is only to prevent Surprize, not to hold to Bail for on this Action it is not demandable;—The *Ac-etiam* runs thus "And also to a Bill of the said A Against the said B for £200 of Debt upon Recognizance. The Ac-etiam Clause is a signal for the Sheriff to Require Bail. in the other Instances[125]

------

[122] Hamilton appears to have ignored the distinction he made *supra* at pp. [27]-[28] between actions bailable of course and actions bailable only by a judge's order. Generally, if damages were certain and exceeded a requisite minimum sum, an *ac etiam* would issue of course, as Hamilton states. Where damages were not easily ascertainable before trial, a judge's order was required. Jacob, *Law Dictionary* (1756 ed.), title "Bail"; Wyche, *NY Supreme Court Practice* (2d ed. 1794) 29.

[123] An Act for prevention of Vexations and Oppressions by Arrests and of Delays in Suits of Law, 13 Car 2, Stat 2, c. 2 (1661).

[124] Hamilton places in quotes standard language for writs. This phrasing was adapted directly from English practice. For contemporary English forms which are substantially identical, see 1 Crompton, *Practice of Common Pleas* (1783) 8. For equally similar colonial forms, see William Livingston, *Lawyer's Precedent Book* (Ms. NYSL, c. 1760) 31.

[125] The words *in the other Instances* are written in an unknown handwriting.

In Actions on a Bail Bond you have no Ac-etiam, the Writ is simply, "to answer to AB Assignee of (the Sheriffs Name) of a Plea of Trespass."—

You Afterwards however declare in Debt and you Recover the whole Penalty on which at your Peril in Equity, you [131] levy what you conceive justly due you with Costs; you indorse Principal, Interest & Costs on the Execution as a Guide to Sheriff which is done in all Cases of Penal Bonds.—

I do not see why the Matter should be left at the Discretion of the Plaintiff, because the Law authorizes the Court to make such Rules on the Bail Bond Suit as they deem most proper for Substantial Justice, and that those Rules shall operate as a Defeazance; Now on this I think the Court may require the Plaintiff to make appear to them the Amount of his Demand either by executing an Inquiry or by entering into Proof to the Court.—[126]

[132]   NOTICE

Whenever four Terms have elapsed without Process, the Defendant must have a whole Terms Notice for the next Step he is to take, as if Declaration be not delivered till four Terms After the Return of the Writ, there must be a Terms Notice to plead; If Trial after Issue joined has been delayed four Terms, there must be a Terms Notice of Trial, but this Terms Notice does not Include Vacation.—

It may be given before the first Day of the Term for the Assizes in Vacation; also you may save the necessity of a whole Terms Notice of Trial, when Circumstances induce a delay by giving Notice of Trial within the four Terms & contermanding the same.—This operates like suing out a Writ to save the Statute of Limitations.—

In England all Motions for Judgment *are Nisi Causa* and four Day Rules, probably it is so here; you actually move [133] for Judgment in Nisi prius

---

[126] Subsequent New York State leqislation achieved the result for which Hamilton argues: ". . . and the court where the action is brought may by rule of the same court give such relief to the plaintiff and defendant in the original action, and bail upon the said bond or other security taken from such bail, as is agreeable to justice; and such rules of the said court shall have the nature and effect of a defeazance of such bail bond or other security for bail." An Act for the Amendment of the Law, and the better Advancement of Justice, *NY Laws*, 24th Sess 1801, c. 90, sec. 8.

Cuses; but in Bar Causes the Motion is understood, and there four Days from the giving of the Verdict, for moving a new Trial or in Arrest of Judgment.—[127]

TENDER

The general Rule for the Cases in which you can make a Tender is, where the Duty or Demand arises on a Thing of an ascertainable Value.—

Yet what is to me incomprehensible, it is said you cannot make a Tender in Debt which of all Actions is the most definite; but perhaps this Rule of Common Law means, that you cannot tender the sum in the Condition, After Penalty has been Incurred by a Forfeiture; but even this is no longer the Case, for the Stat. 4 & 5 Ann which adopted by an Act of our [134] Legislature (vide Laws of N.Y. 1769)[128] anytime pending the Action Tender of the Principal with Interest and Costs will put an End to the suit; And no

---

[127] In England, only in King's Bench was a motion for judgment required. In both King's Bench and Common Pleas the defendant had four days in which to move for a new trial or in arrest of judgment. Wood, *Institutes* (10th ed. 1772) 600. In 1794 in New York both on circuit and at bar a motion had to be made for judgment, and the rule was for four days. Wyche, *NY Supreme Court Practice* (2d ed. 1794) 187.

[128] The colonial enactment which adopted the English Statute 4 & 5 Anne (An Act for the Amendment of the Law and the better Advancement of Justice, 4 & 5 Anne, c. 3, sec. 12 [1705]) was entitled "An Act to declare the Extension of several Acts of Parliament made since the Establishment of a Legislation in this Colony: and not declared in the said Act to extend to the Plantations." 4 *Col Laws NY* 954 (1767). This act was disallowed by the King in Council in 1770. As a law student in 1782, Hamilton regarded the act as having had sufficient vitality to have been the basis of reception into New York law of the statute 4 & 5 Anne. Section thirty-five of the 1777 New York State Constitution declared: ". . . That such parts of the common law of England and Great-Britain, and of the colony of New-York, as did together form the law of the said colony on the nineteenth day of April, in the year of our Lord, one thousand seven hundred and seventy-five, shall be and continue the law in this state. . . ." Because this 1767 act was vetoed in 1770 it was not extant law on April 19, 1775, and within the terms of the reception provision of the constitution should not have been received as part of New York law, and therefore could not have provided a basis for the adoption of the statute 4 & 5 Anne. Hamilton was probably unaware that the act had been disallowed. Van Schaak printed only the title and stated that the act had been disallowed. Since Hamilton's reference indicates he had seen the text of the act in an edition of the laws prior to Van Schaak's compilation, he presumably assumed the act to be in force. Late in the decade in which Hamilton wrote *Practical Proceedings* at least two New York lawyers were aware that the status of colonial legislation (not to mention disallowed colonial legislation) might cause difficulties. In a preface to their 1789 edition of the *Laws of New York*, Samuel Jones and Richard Varick stated, ". . . several of the public Acts of the late Colony, could not, with any Degree of Propriety, be reenacted or repealed. These Acts still continue to form Part of the Law of the State. There are others, of general Concern, which altho' repealed, or became obsolete by new provisions, must give the Rule relative to Things done before. . . ."

doubt I should Imagine where the Debt is on single Bond tender may be made; yet the Books seem to speak a different Language.—

It is a General Rule that in Trespass you cannot tender because the Damages are uncertain and depend on the Judgment of the Jury. By Statute[129] however, tender of Amends is Allowed in Trespass *quare clausum fregit*, and in Case of a wrongful Distress, with more Reason they may be allowed *de bonis asportatis*. So in Trover unless for Money; but the Spirit of some late Decisions makes this Questionable. In a Case Reported by Burrows 3 Vol.[130] it is laid down *arguendo* that in Trover whenever the Goods are of an [135] ascertainable Value and have not been altered in Quality or Form, and the taking or Conversion of them is not attended with some aggravation Circumstances proper to enhance the Damages, they may be brought into Court. The Reason of this applies with additional Force to tender of their Value in which there can be no Difficulty.

A Tender on a *Quantum meruit* is allowed and altho I have seen no Authorities to the Effect, I should Suppose for the same Reason, a Tender on a *Quantum Valebat* should be good, it is understood; so on an *Indebitatus Assumpsit* on an express Agreement; or an *insimul computasset*.—

A Tender must be the full Value; for if it is anything less it will not be good; It must be made also before the Action commences, for it is too late Afterwards.—

[136] If a Tender has been made it must be pleaded in Bar, averring that you have been always Ready and are still Ready to pay &c: You must at the same Time make a *Profert in Curia* of the Money, otherwise the Plea will not be good.—

BRINGING MONEY INTO COURT

This is done when you have Neglected to make a Tender beforehand and you wish to pay the Plaintiff his Due and save the Costs by Staying farther

---

[129] An Acte for lymytacon of Accons, and for avoyding of Suits in Lawe, 21 Jac 1, c. 16, sec. 5 (1623-1624).

[130] Fisher v. Prince, 3 Burr. 1363 (KB 1762).

Proceedings. This may be done in all Cases where a Tender might have been made.—

The Rule is that it ought to be done before Plea pleaded, but there are Instances of its having been done after Issue Joined and the Plaintiff not [137] having lost a Trial, so as to leave the Plaintiff in no worse Situation than before. The manner of doing it is this[131] you move the Court for leave to bring such a sum of Money into Court, to discharge so much of the Plaintiffs Demand as is just; upon which the Court will make a Rule granting Leave, and I imagine ordering that if the Plaintiff accepts it as a full Satisfaction, then all further Proceedings to be staid, but if he does not accept it, then so much to be struck out of the Declaration; and if on Trial of the Issue more be found due to him than is tendered, that he shall Recover Costs if not, that then he shall pay Costs to the Defendant. (not having seen the Rule this is only conjecture).—[132]

The Defendant Immediately send a [138] Copy of this Rul[e] accompanied with the General Issue to the Plaintiff, and if, he proceeds it is at the Hazard of Costs.—

Analogous to this is pleading Payment by an Act of our Legislature;[133] you may sett off any Debt or Duty against another by pleading Payment in Bar, and giving Notice in Writing of what you intend to sett off.[134] If more is due you than you owe the Plaintiff, the Jury will certify the Overplus, and it

---

[131] Comparison of this manner of bringing money into court with the tender provision in New York's latest civil procedure revision (which became effective September 1, 1963) indicates that the new law is antedated by New York practice of nearly 200 years ago. Civil Procedure Law and Rules, rule 3219, *NY Laws,* 1962, c. 308. The new statute is restricted to contract actions and does not require court approval.

[132] Such statements as "I imagine ordering that if the Plaintiff accepts it as a full Satisfaction" and "not having seen the Rule this is only conjecture" have, as noticed, led the editors to conclude that the author of the Practice Manual was a student of law and not a practicing lawyer at the time he wrote. It appears that Hamilton was correct in his conjecture as to the form of a rule ordering money paid into court. For such a rule of the New York Supreme Court in 1807, see Caines, *A Summary of the Practice of the Supreme Court of the State of New York* (1808) 169.

[133] 5 *Col Laws NY* 540 (1773).

[134] Hamilton was referring to "An Act for the Relief of Insolvent Debtors within the Colony of New York with respect to the Imprisonment of their persons" (which had a provision for set-off). 5 *Col Laws NY* 120, 125 (1770). This act was extended in 1771, but expired in 1772 and thereafter was not reenacted until 1788. An Act for the Amendment of the Law, and the better Advancement of Justice, *NY Laws,* 11 Sess 1788, c. 46, sec. 1. It was not uncommon for the procedure authorized by a colonial act to be continued in practice after the act had become obsolete. See *supra* n. 128.

will become a Debt of Record against the Plaintiff, for which you may have a Sci: fa:—

If the Sett off does not equal the Plaintiffs Demand, you may bring the Pallance into Court on the Common Rule and Oblige the Plaintiff to Proceed at his Parel; this may be deduced from the English Practice combined with ours.—[135]

[139]   JURIES

The Proper Province of the Jury is to determin[e] Matters of Fact not of Law; but they may at their Peril determine both; and it often happens that the Law and Fact are so blanded that they cannot be separated.—

Juries may be challenged; challenges are first divided into two Heads, challenges to the Array & Challenges to the Polls; Challenges to the Array are to be made when the Officer is not to be considered as impartial.—

Where he is related in the ninth Degree.

When he is Interested in the Cause.

When he has been guilty of any unfair Proceeding has Received a Bribe or the like.—

Challenges to the Polls are where, tho' no Objection can be made to the Array the Jurors themselves may labour under some Disqualifications, *propter affectum* [140] *propter defectum, propter delictum* or in Case of,

Relationship in the ninth Degree as above.

Being interested in the Cause.

Having been an Arbitrator or Jury in the Cause.

Being an Infant or Ideot, or of non sane Memory.

Being above or under legal Age.

---

[135] Compare 3 Blackstone, *Commentaries* (Phila. ed. 1771) 304, and An Act for the Relief of Debtors with respect to the Imprisonment of their Persons, 2 Geo 2, c. 22, sec. 13 (1729) (made permanent and amended by An Act to explain and amend an Act passed in the second year of the Reign of his present Majesty, intituled, *An Act for the Relief of Debtors with Respect to the Imprisonment of their Persons,* c. 46, sec. 1 [1788]) with Wyche, *NY Supreme Court Practice* (2d ed. 1794) 119, 120, and *NY Laws,* 11th Sess 1788, c. 46, sec. 1. Similarity of phrasing indicates that the drafters of the New York statute had the English statutes before them.

Not having the Necessary Qualifications of Property.

Being an Alien, except in Juries *de med. Lingua*[136]

Having been attainted or convicted of some infamous Crime.—

Felony, Perjury, Fraud &c: in order to make them Principal challenges, the Record of Conviction must be produced; if not they are only Challenges to the Favor." But it is said that after Pardon, then Stigmas go only to the Credit, not to the Sufficiency of the Witness.—

Challenges are again divided into principal Challenges & Challenges to the Favor. All the Forementioned Heads are Principal Cause of Challenge. Challenges to the [141] Favor, are connection beyond the ninth Degree by Blood, connections by Marriage, particular Connections in Trade &c: whenever unattended with an Interest in the Particular Thing in Dispute.—

The being a Debtor Tenant &c: to either of the Parties, indeed the being a Tenant is sometimes ranked among principal Causes. These and a variety of Other Particulars are Challenges to the Favor. Principal Challenges when once the Fact be admitted, incapacitate absolutely.—

Challenges to the Favor are submitted to the Decision of Triors, who Judge whether the Grounds of the Challenge be Sufficient, to produce a Strong Presumption of Partiality, or not, & admit or Reject accordingly.—

When a Challenge is made if it be a Principal one, and the Fact be not [142] Disputed or if the Challenge be to the Favor, the Court will Appoint Triors who are commonly two Attornies; who examine Witnesses and decide upon the Sufficiency. If the Challenges are to the Polls and there are two Jurors already sworn, they will be Triors, if there are not, two other Triors will be appointed; and when one Sufficient Juror is sworn he will be joined to them; when two are Admitted, they alone try the Subsequent Challenges.—

The Triors are sworn & authorised to examine Witnesses, or any Document proper to establish the Facts contested.—

When the Jurors are sworn they must have no Conversation or Intercourse with any Person whatever, they must not leave the Bar without

---

[136] Some of the grounds for challenges which Hamilton lists may have been taken from 3 Blackstone, *Commentaries* (Phila. ed. 1771) 361-366, 4 Blackstone, *Commentaries* (Phila. ed. 1771) 346-348, or from 1 Coke, *Institutes* (11th ed. 1719) 156-159.

Leave of the Court or without the Attendance of a Consta-[143]ble. When they Leave the Bar they must have Communication with no one except to say whether they have or have not agreed upon their Verdict; they may Neither eat nor drink nor have Fire or Candle without Leave of the Court. If they eat or drink at their own Expence this is fineable; If at the Expence of the Party for whom they find it vitiates their Verdict.—

If they Cast Lots or throw Dice or by any other Hazard determine the Cause, the Verdict is bad.

When Attaints were in Use Juries were Permitted to give private parol Evidence, not produced on the Trial, to each other; this was an Indulgence to save them from the Imputation of Perjury, and the terrible Consequences of an Attaint. But now Attaints are disused, it is no longer Allowable though some Authorities still say, they may give Writings in Evidence to each other. (vide Bathurst Trials [144] at Nisi prius.)—[137]

To Attaints has succeeded new Trials which will be allowed in all Cases of Misbehaviour in the Jury, Misdirection of the Judge, when the Jury have mistaken the Law, or the Verdict is palpably against Evidence, or the Damages excessive, or when the Judge has Refused to admit proper Evidence, or has Overruled some legal Right of the Party. With an Inconsistancy common in the Law, though new Trials are common for excessive Damages, they are not allowed for too small Damages. But the Court will grant a new Inquiry when the Damages are inadequate or Excessive; the Reason Assigned is that these are merely in the Nature of an Inquest of Office for Informing the Conscience of the Judges, & they might without an Inquest have assessed the Damages.

For the same Reason the Court will [145] increase or mitigate the Damages given by Juries of Inquiry which they will not do in Juries of Trial except in flagrant Cases of Battery or Maham, where upon Inspection of the Wound and Certificate of the Judge, that it was the same proved on the Trial, the Court if they think the Damages Insufficient, will increase them, for the same Reason there are no Challenges to Juries of Inquiry and for the like Reason they may be adjourned from time to Time You give the same Notices for Executing Writs of Inquiry as for Trials, but you must be as particular as

---

[137] 2 Bathurst, *Introduction to the Law Relative to Trials at Nisi Prius* (1768 ed.) 293.

possible in describing the place &c. You must specify between such an Hour & such an Hour, Allowing two Hours.—

To avoid the Inconveniances of a Challenge to the Array, in Case the Sheriff is under any disability suggest it to the Court & pray that a Venire be awarded to the Coroner; if the Coroner is exceptionable [146] This must also be suggested, and a Venire prayed to Elizors (two indifferent Persons Appointed by the Court). If the Defendant disputes the Matter he will be precluded from Challenging the Array; if this is not done the Defendant when the Day of Trial arrives after the Jurors Names are called over and before any of them are sworn makes his Challenge in Writing, something in the following Form, "And now at this Day comes AB and Challenges the Array, for that CD Esquire Sheriff of the County of _____ is Cousin to the said EF" (setting forth particularly the Relationship) or for any other Cause as above. This the Defendant may traverse in Nature of a Replication; and Triors are appointed if it be not a Principal Challenge, as before mentioned; I think I have seen it laid down in *Law of Evidence*,[138] that the Defendant may Challenge for [147] Relationship to himself as well as the Plaintiff but these Authorities to the Contrary, it is held in our Courts that he can.

Elisors cannot be Challenged if after Appointment they are found ever so much interested. Challenges After Venire returned as to the Array do never appear upon the Record; but Challenges before Venire Issues to the Sheriff, Coroner &c: are always entered on the Roll.—

On the Act of Wm. 3d.[139] if you obtain Judgment on *Demurrer*, or by *Confession Default* &c: there must still a Jury come before the Court or the Judges of *Nisi prius* to inquire into the Truth of the Breaches, as well as to Assess the Quantum of Damages. Laws of N.Y. 640.—[140]

---

[138] Gilbert, *The History and Practice of the Court of Common Pleas* (1st ed. 1737) 79.

[139] An Act for the better preventing frivolous and vexatious Suits, 8 & 9 Will 3, c. 11, sec. 8 (1696-1697).

[140] An Act for the better preventing frivolous and vexatious Suits, 5 *Col Laws NY* 289-290. The work Hamilton cited was 1 *Laws of New York from the Year 1691 to 1773 inclusive* (NY Hugh Gaine 1774).

[148]   RELEASE

The most effectual Release is by Writing under Seal, by which the Releasor, "remises Releases and quits Claim to all Actions, Suits, Debts, Dues & Demands whatsoever, from the Beginning of the World to the present Day of the Release.—

By a Release of all Actions, you not only Release all such Things as are depending in Courts of Justice or Equity, but all such things as are *debitum in presenti*, or due at the Time, which have not received the Judgment of a Court of Justice. It does not release Executions. It releases a Bond with A Penalty with Condition in *futuro*, for this is *Debitum in presenti solvendum in futuro*.—

A Release of all Suits Releases all Executions, but a Release of all Demands is of a larger Extent than either, it releases not only what is Debitum in presenti, but [149] which is *Debitum in futuro*, upon a Transaction existing in *presenti*. It releases all Actions Judgments & Executions. It releases a Rent Charge, but not a Rent Service, tho' there is no satisfactory Reason for this Distinction.—

It is a Rule in Releases, that general Words shall be taken strictly against the Releasor; except where they are qualified by some Special Recital.—

Formerly Courts were very strict in following the Words of a Release, and their legal Import but latterally they take into Consideration the apparent Intention of the Parties, and will favor that against the Generality of the Release. vide Bacon Title Release.[141]

A Release to one of joint, or joint & several Obligors is a Release to the whole & a Release by one of the Joint Obligees is a Release of the whole. A Covenant (where there is only one [150] Obligor) not to sue, indefinitely, is an Absolute Release; but it is not so if it be for a limited Time, and if Covenantor before the Time sues, the Covenant cannot be pleaded in Bar but the Party must bring an Action of Covenant for the Release. So where there are Joint Obligees, a Covenant not to sue one is not a Release.—

A Release may be pleaded in Bar, but an Acquittance cannot but you may give it in Evidence. The Difference between them is, that the former is a sealed Instrument, the letter an unsealed one.—

---

[141] 4 Bacon, *A New Abridgment of the Law* (3d ed. 1768) 289.

It is held as a general Rule, that you cannot release Choses in Action, mere Possibility and Contingences; yet you can release a Bond, *solvendum in futuro,* which is a Chose in Action Indeed I do not understand the Rule, so far as it applies to Choses in Action, for it seems in Fact that they are all Releaseable; and the proper Objects of a Release.[142] It is said Choses in Action are only introduced Collaterally, as not being assignable, rather then not releaseable.—

[151]   COVENANT

Is an Instrument under Seal by which a Person binds himself, to do or not to do a Certain Thing.—

Any Word of Stipulation or Agreement, without the Word *Covenant,* will amount to a Covenant. There are two Kinds of Covenants, Covenant in Deed & Covenant in Law; Covenant in Deed is, where the express Words

---

[142] Hamilton relied heavily on Bacon's *Abridgment* in this section. The source of his "general Rule" about release of a chose in action is probably the following passage: "It is a general Rule in our Books that a mere Possibility cannot be released, and the Reason hereof is, that a Release supposeth a Right in Being, and it was thought to countenance Maintenance to transfer Choses in Action, Possibilities and Contingent Interests." 4 Bacon, *A New Abridgment of the Law* (3d ed. 1768) 283.

Perhaps Hamilton did not understand the rule because he had overlooked a subtitle in the abridgment ("How far a Possibility or Contingent Interest may be released") which restricted the application of Bacon's general rule to those choses in action which were possibilities or contingent interests. After Hamilton had incorrectly paraphrased Bacon's rule to state that no chose in action could be released, it was natural that he should have been puzzled, for by the law of that time many choses in action were releasable. Bacon, *op. cit. supra* at 283-289; 1 Coke, *Institutes* (11th ed. 1719) 264-295; 2 Lilly, *Abridgment* (pt. 2, 1735) 533-539. Another probable source of Hamilton's misunderstanding is that although he rephrased the distinctions made by Bacon concerning release of actions and release of demands, and concerning present and future debts, he seems to have missed what was an important distinction for choses in action: that presently existing debts owing in the future could be released, while those not presently existing, but contingent upon a subsequent event, could not. The examples provided by Bacon do not evince any clear rationale for establishing a dividing line between contingent and noncontingent choses in action. A bond "conditioned to pay Money at a Day to come" was releasable, while "an Action of Debt for Non-performance of an Award made for the Payment of Money at a Day to come" was not, according to Bacon, *op. cit. supra* at 286. The case which Bacon cites for the latter situation enunciates some seventeenth-century English line-drawing principles. Bridges v. Einon, Yelv. 214 (KB 1612). However, if Hamilton did consult this case while studying Bacon's *Abridgment,* his difficulty in formulating a rule for release of choses in action was further complicated, for Bacon misstated the holding of the case, which in fact held that the award in question could be released prior to the date on which the money was to be paid. Substantive errors in popular works like Bacon's *Abridgment,* Blackstone's *Commentaries,* and Coke's *Institutes* were not uncommon, and posed hazards to clients, lawyers, and students of law.

import a Covenant, Covenant in Law is, where it arises only by necessary Implications, or where it is transferred by some Subsequent Act or Event to a third Person.—

It is said a Covenant in Law cannot be of a Thing not in *esse* at the Time of entering into it; as if a Lessor Covenants to build an House upon the Premises and Assigns, the Covenant ~~with~~ will not run with the Lands and bind the Assignee. But in a late Case reported in 3 Burrows[143] it was held, that if the Covenant had been to Build [152] an House in a Limited time, and the Time had Expired, and Afterwards the Premises haid been Assigned, the Assignee would not have been bound, but if the Time had not Expired he would have been bound.—

When there are mutual Covenants the Breach of one cannot be pleaded in Bar of an Action for the Beach of the others, but each must bring his Action.—

In an Action on a Penal Bond Conditioned for the Performance of Covenants, you are allowed by Statutes[144] to suggest as many Breaches as you Please, and the Jury will find Accordingly. If the Party tenders Satisfaction for the Damages it will stay the Proceedings, but Judgment will be entered for the Penalty, and remain a Security for future Breaches; on the happening of which you bring a *Sci: fa:* upon the Judgment [153] and are allowed to suggest the Breaches on the Roll. If you Obtain Judgment on Demurrer, by Confession, Default &c: there must still a Jury come before the Court, or the Judge at *Nisi prius*, to inquire into the Truth of the Breaches as well as to assess Damages.—

The Practitioners differ concerning the Manner of Assigning your Breaches; in the first Instance some say it ought to be done in the Declaration, others that your Declaration ought to be a simple Declaration in Debt for the Penalty, that Defendant Craves Oyer of the Deed whereupon it is Read and become part of the Declaration, that he then Pleads Performance, and that

---

[143] Churchwardens of St. Savior's Southwark v. Smith, 3 Burr. 1273 (KB 1762).

[144] An Act for the better preventing frivolous and vexatious Suits, 8 & 9 Will 3, c. 11, sec. 8 (1696-1697), received by an Act to declare the Extension of several Acts of Parliament made since the Establishment of a Legislation in this Colony: and not declared in the said Act to extend to the Plantations, 4 *Col Laws NY* 953, 954 (1767) (disallowed by King in Council 1770). Again, Hamilton makes reference to disallowed colonial legislation as if it were currently effective law. See *supra* n. 128.

the Plaintiff in his Replication sets forth the Breaches, which being traversed by the Defendant, brings them to Issue & Trial. The Judgment on this Action is for the Penalty & for the Damages Assessed. When the Damages Justify the Penalty you must proceed no farther; for the Penalty was the Compensation intended for the Breach of the whole Covenant, & you cannot exceed it.—

[154]   LIMITATIONS

These by Statutes[145] with respect to the Actions now in use are, in Ejectment 20 Years; If a Person on Ancestors from whom he Claims has not had Possession within 20 Years last past, his Right of Entry is barred, and he cannot bring an Action of Ejectment. But as has been already Observed, there has been a late Decision over-turning this as far as its Authority may be allowed. vide Burrows.—[146]

Also if there has been a Discent after 5 years peaceable Possession, from the Disseisor, tho' no more time has elapsed, it bars the Right of Entry.—

Most personal Actions must be brought within Six Years after the Cause of Action has Arisen: from this are excepted, all specialties; and Current Accounts between Marchants.—

Actions of Imprisonment, Assault & [155] Battery must be brought within four Years.—

Actions for Words must be brought within two Years, but this is where the Words are in themselves actionable: for where they are only consequentially so by Means of some special Damage which is the Gist of the Action, they are not within the Statute. (Bathurst).—[147]

---

[145] Wrongfull disseasyn to be descente, 32 Hen 8, c. 33 (1540); An Acte for lymytacon of Accons, and for avoyding of Suits in Lawe, 21 Jac 1, c. 16, secs. 1 & 3 (1623-1624); An Act for the Amendment of the Law and the better Advancement of Justice, 4 & 5 Anne, c. 3 (1705); An Act to declare the Extension of several Acts of Parliament made since the Establishment of a Legislation in this Colony: and not declared in the said Act to extend to the Plantations, 4 *Col Laws NY* 954 (1767) (vetoed by King in Council 1770).

[146] Probably Winchelsea Causes, 4 Burr. 1963 (KB 1766) (dictum).

[147] Bathurst, *Introduction to the Law Relative to Trials at Nisi Prius* (1768) 6.

Actions on Penal Statutes, if the Penalty is wholly, or partly to the sovereign in two years;**148** if to the Prosecutor, in one.—

But the Statute of Limitations may be saved by suing out, before the Expiration of the Time, a Bill or Capias and get it Returned Non est Inventus, entering it on the Roll, and continuing it Down till the Process Actually served. vide Attys. Guide 49, 50.—**149**

[156]   FORCIBLE ENTRY & DETAINER

When a Person makes a forcible entry upon the Poss[ess]ion of an other, or after a Peaceable Entry unlawfully keeps Possession by Force, a Justice upon a Representation, taking with him another Justice by Way of Precaution will go to the Premises, and if he sees actual signs of Subsisting Force, he is Authorized to Fine the Persons and Commit them until they pay the Fine; if after Committing them the Possession is vacant, the Injured Party may enter and take Possession.—

But if there is no Subsisting Force he must summon a Jury of 24 to have an Inquest of the Force, giving Notice to the Parties of the Time & Place. When the Jury is Assembled, if they Find the Force, he may then   the Disseisor and Restore the [157] Rightful Possession, unless the Desseisor Pleads three Years previous Possession, or traverses the Force; in which Case he must summon a Jury of 12 to try the Fact, and if they find against the Deforcer the Justices are Authorized to dispossess him in Favor of the Rightful Possessor. The first a Criminal Proceeding, and the Jury in Nature of an Inquest of Office, the latter in Nature of a Jury of Trial.—

---

148 Hamilton was mistaken. The statute of limitations was two years only if the penalty went wholly to the sovereign; one year if it went partly to the sovereign; one year if wholly to the prosecutor. An Acte Concerninge Informers, 31 Eliz 1, c. 5, sec. 5 (1588). Colonial and early state legislation contains no New York enactment which might have modified the English law to read as Hamilton stated it. In 1788 New York enacted a statue with provisions substantially similar in this regard to those of Stature 31 Eliz 1, c. 5, sec. 5. An Act for the Limitation of Criminal Prosecutions, and of Actions and Suits at Law, *NY Laws,* 11 Sess 1788, c. 43, sec. 8.

149 *The Attorney's Compleat Guide in the Court of King's Bench by an attorney of the court* (London 1773) 49, 50.

[158]   AUDITA QUERELA

Is a Writ issuing out of Chancery stating particularly the Nature of the Complaint materially requiring the Court, to hear the Complaint of the Party, and what both have to say for themselves, and do therein what shall seem to them Just. The Praecipe for this Writ must be much in Details. Attys. Guide 273.—[150]

It issues chiefly when after Judgment any Fact turns up which ought to prevent Execution or if Execution has taken place ought to procure Restitution; also in some Cases when before Judgment, pending the Action, if from Circumstances the Party had it not in his Power to avail himself the Matter by a Plea *puis darein continuance,* for if he had an Opportunity of availing himself of it, an *audita Querela,* will not be allowed. In many Cases the Courts will relieve on Motion, which says Blackstone,[151] has driven the *audita querela* almost intirely out of [159] Practice. But where the Fact is susceptable of Dispute the Court will not Relieve on Motion, and then the only legal Remedy is by *audita querela.*—

After suing out the Writ you pray the Court that it may be Read & filed, and after Reading that it may be allowed; after Allowance you pray that the Clerk may Indorse the Allowance upon it and then you move for Leave to put in Bail, and afterwards for a Supersedeas.—

It is said if the *Audita Querela* be founded upon a Release or Matter of Record, then Bail will be allowed, but not if it be founded on a Surmise of Fact only; Yet there is an Authority in Jacobs Law Dictionary,[152] by which it appears Bail have been allowed on a Surmise of Fact.—

When the *Audita querela* is founded upon Matters of Record, or the Party is in Custody, you summon the Opposite Party by *Scire facias;* when it is founded on Matter of Pais or the Plaintiff in the *Audita querela* [160] is not in Custody, you proceed by *Venire* and Distress infinite.—

In the Scire facias, probably you set forth the Matter of Complaint particularly, and the Matter proceeds as in othe[r] Cases of Scire facias.—

---

[150] *Id.* at 273.
[151] 3 Blackstone, *Commentaries* (1771 ed.) 405.
[152] Jacob, *A New Law Dictionary,* title "Audita Querela."

The Bail in this Case have no alternative if their Principal was Cast, but paying the Condamnation Money & Costs.

An *audita querela* will be allowed after Sci: fa: with two Nihils, for something that existed before; but it will not be allowed after a Sci: feci returned; this is because in the first Case the Matter may have never come to his knowledge consequently he may never have had an opportunity of making use of the Plea on which the *audita querela* is founded.—

Execution may be sued out not withstanding this Writ till a *Supersedeas* be Obtained which cannot be had until Bail put in, or if grounded on Fact, till the same is proved in Court.—

The Judgment in *audita querela* is That the Plaintiff in Judgment shall not have Execution of his Judgment.—

Note There must be four Bail in *audita querela*.—

[161]   TRESPASS IN EJECTMENT

This is an Action of very great Importance which has succeeded to almost all the old real Actions for the Recovery of Landed Property.—

It is a mixed Action, partly Real & Partly Personal and Recovers not only the Possession of the Thing for which it is brought, but Damages for the Ouster. It is a Creature of Westminster Hall & subsists Chiefly upon Fiction. The general Doctrine is, that this Action could only be brought by a Person who had a Right of entry, and the Manner of Proceeding was this; The Person who intended to bring the Action, and made an Actual Entry upon part of the Premises, and there sealed a Lease, for as many years as was thought conveniant to some Friend and left him in Possession till the Real Tenant or some other person by Agreement, came & turned him out, the first was Called the Lessor, the second the Lessee, and the third the Casual Ejector; This [162] Mode is still followed when the premises are vacant, and an Affidavit is produced in Court, setting forth particularly all the proceedings, that the Court may be able to judge whether they have been Regular & Conformable to the Rule.—It is also followed when a Corporation is the Plaintiff, who appoint & authorize an Attorney, under their Seal, for that Purpose. It is also said to be the best when there are several Claimants, who may not be able to distinguish accurately in Proof, the Parcel to which each lays Claim; and it seems this is not necessary when there is an actual Entry.—

But the general Practice is by a fictitious Lease Entry & Ouster, and managed by the following Contrivance.—

You make out a Declaration setting forth that on a certain Day A made a Demise to B for so many years, that B entered on the Premisses in consequance of the [163] Demise, and was Possessed thereof; that afterwards at a Particular Time C entered & drove him out &c. both B & C fictitious Persons, and Declaration Delivered in Vecation, must be capped of the Preceding Term at the end of your Declaration you write a Notice from C the Casual Ejector, to D, the real Tenant in Possession informing him that an Action of Trespass in Ejectment has been brought against him as casual Ejector; that he having no Title to the Premisses & having heard that D has, Advises him to appear and be made Defendant in his Stead, that otherwise he will suffer Judgment to go against him by Default, and he D will be turned out of Possession this Declaration & Notice you must Deliver to the Tenant [in] Possession, or to his Wife, it will not be good Deliverence to any other Person, unless the Tenant absconds or Conceals himself

[*Marginal addition:*]

It may be left at the house, or stuck up in the door, without leave of Court provided the tenant nor any of his family cannot be found[153]

to avoid it, and you afterwards move the Court, who will give you leave to serve it upon one of his Children, or his Servants, or even [164] to leave it at his House. There are Instances in such Cases where the Delivery has been held good on Affidavit of the Reason, without the Previous Leave of the Court; but it is safest to Obtain it.—

In the Term following you Inform the Court that a Declaration has been Delivered in a Cause of Trespass in Ejectment, to D, and pray that the Notice & Affidavit of Delivery may be read & filed. The Affidavit that must be made for this purpose must specify precisely, that the Declaration and Notice annexed, were delivered to the Tenant in Possession, or to the Person who

---

[153] In different handwriting but apparently inserted in the margin by the same person who made the insertion on p. [167]. This person is hereafter cited as person "B."

Acknowledges himself Tenant in Possession, or to the Wife of the Tenant in Possession.—

When the Notice & Affidavit have been read, you then move the Court for a Rule, that unless the Tenant in Possession will appear, and be made Defendant instead of the Casual Ejector, that then [165] there may be Judgment against the Casual Ejector; this Rule will be granted accordingly.—

If the Tenant in Possession does not appear, in the Term following you move for Judgment *nisi causa* (or unless the Tenant in Possession will appear) for want of a Plea, against the Casual Ejector, which will be granted of Course. This is a four Days Rule.—

You then make up your Judgment Roll with an Award of Execution and take out a Writ of *Habere Facias Possessionem* accordingly.—

You may afterwards have an Action of Trespass if you please, against the Tenant in Possession for the mesne profits; in this Action you also recover your Costs in the first action; but you have in this Case no other Remedy for them; the Lessee here must go into the Proof of his Title.—

But if the Tenant in Possession has a Mind to defend his Title, ~~you~~ he must appear According to the Rule in 20 Days after the [166] End of the Term. He appears by filing common Bail, & then calls upon the Plaintiffs Atty, receives a Declaration & then enters into the common Rule for Confessing Lease Entry & Ouster.[154] The common Rule is Signed by the Attorneys on both Sides; and on the common Rule the Defendant pleads the general Issue, *not guilty* the Declaration must be altered by inserting the Tenant in Possession, instead of the Casual Ejector; also in the Margin of the Common Rule you write the premises in Question as mentioned in the Declaration, next follows the Trial as in other Cases.

If the Tenant afterwards make Default or Refuses to Confess Lease Entry & Ouster, according to the purport of the Rule, the Plaintiff must be nonprossed; but Judgment may be afterwards entered against the Casual Ejector by Default. Note on the Trial you call on the Defendant to Confess [167] Lease Entry & Ouster; if he does not appear to confess Lease Entry & Ouster the Plaintiff is then nonsuited; but he will Obtain Judgment by Default against the Casual Ejector as above mentioned, and will of Course

[154] See Exhibit CC.

recover his Possession and also his Costs; in order to which the Defendant must be served with a taxed Bill thereof & a Copy of the common Rule the Original being shewn to him at the same Time, and if he does not upon this pay Costs, on Motion founded on Affidavit of the Particulars the Court will grant an Attachment. When the Matter is determined by Verdict the Plaintiff may have a Ca: sa: or a Fi: fa: for his Costs. If Judgment goes against the *Plaintiff*,[155] the Tenant has his ~~Defendant~~ [155] Remedy against the Lessor; that is by serving the common Rule & Attacment. If the Lessor be an Infant the Court will stay proceedings till competent Security be given for Costs.—

The Remedy for mesne Profits in this [168] Case as well as in the former, must be by an Action of the Trespass on the Case; you recover from the Time of the Ouster laid in the Declaration, and if the Action be brought by the nominal Plaintiff you need not go into a Proof of Title; but if by the Lessor himself you must do it if it is insisted upon or controverted, some late authorities reject his Opinion, and with propriety.—

If there are several Plaintiffs who have several Interests, there must be several Demises laid in the Declaration, otherwise it will be erroneous, but if there is a joint Interest, as in Case of joint Tenants and Coparceners, one Demise will suffice.—

Also if there are several Tenants in Possession a seperate Declaration must be delivered to each, tho' they may be consolidated in the Action.—

When they enter into the common Rule and they have several Interests, it would be proper that each should give you a Note [169] in Writing for the Particular Parcel to which he claims Title, otherwise you could be obliged to distinguish the particular Parcels in Proof, which might be difficult. If the Defendant will not do this voluntarily, you must get a Judges Summons for them to have the common Rule drawn up specially, designating the several Parcels, for which they respectively defend.—

If on the Trial some of the Defendants make a Default, and others appear, the Plaintiff must be nonprossed as to those who do not appear but the Trial may proceed as to the others, & it must be indorsed on the *Postea*,

---

[155] Person "B" (see n. 153, *supra*) inserted the word *Defendant* (thereafter crossed-out) in the margin, possibly to replace the word *Plaintiff*, lightly underscored in the parallel line of text.

that the Nonpross was for Want of their Appearance to confess Lease, Entry & Ouster; and Judgment with Respect to them will go against the Casual Ejector.—

Note, *In Barnes*[156] The Judges hint a Disapprobation of the Practice of having [170] seperate Action for the mesne Profits, either they say, might as well be recovered in the first Action, and doubtless this is agreeable to the primitive Design of the Action, and Would be most convenient, as well as most agreeable to the Maxims of the Law; that the Law abhors Circuity, or multiplicity of Actions." However, the Course of Authorities is for seperate Actions.

Any Landlord may be made a *Co-Defendant* in this Action if the Tenant Refuses to appear and will be admitted in his stead; even after Judgment has gone against the Casual Ejector on Payment of Costs, entering into the common Rule and taking short Notice of Trial.—This Motion to the Court for Admission, in the last Case, must be founded on Affidavit, setting forth, that he called upon the Tenant in Possession to defend, and offered to indamnify him for the Costs, but that he utterly refused.

[171] It has been held till lately, that no Person can be made Defendant but he who was, or had at the Time been in Possession, or who was in the Receipt of Rent: but this in a late Case reported in Burrows[157] seems to have been over ruled, as well as the Doctrine of the Necessity of a Right of Entry to qualify a Lessor; for then Persons Claiming Escheat after an Extinction of Heirs were admitted. It is there also held that it is not necessary to prove an actual Entry, but in Case to avoid a Fine. It has formerly been held necessary between Tenants in Common. In Case the Tenant in Possession should be a material Witness he must not appear, and then the Landlord getting himself admitted, may make a Witness of him; for if the Tenant has once appeared, the Court will not afterwards release him, to become a Witness.—

[172] In Ejectment there are several Niceties about the Time of laying the Ouster, if the Demise is Stated at the 10th. of April, to have & to hold from this Day, for it is held this will be before the Title of the Lessee com-

---

[156] Barnes, *Notes of Cases in Points of Practice* (1754) 159 (Treherne v. Greffingham [CP 1742] [dictum]).
[157] Fair-claim, *ex dimiss'* Fowler *et al.* v. Sham-title, 3 Burr. 1290 (KB 1761).

menced, which in this case was not till the Eleventh; but if it had been said, to have & to hold from thence forth, the Lease would have been the same Day, but for fear of Mistakes it is better to lay it some Day after.—

It is said the Declaration being in Nature of a Writ, the Court will not allow it to be altered; but there are Authorities of Instances, in which they have suffered the Term to be lengthened; however the Propriety of this is Disputed, and it is best to run no Risque by laying a Sufficient Lease at first. It is difficult however to conceive when it is required by a Rule of Kings Bench, that you take out a Bill or Latitat & file common Bail before you file Declaration If Notice of Trial has been given in the Cause & not countermanded in Time, so that Costs are incurred, these must be paid before the Court will proceed on a Second Notice.—

By a particular Statute (11 Geo. 2.)[158] the Tenant in Possession must give immediate Notice of [173] any Declaration served upon him, to his landlord, on pain of forfeiting three years Rent. Also the landlord has in this Action Strong security for his Rent; if upon the Lease he has reserved the Right of Entry & there is half a years Rent in arreare, even without any previous Demand, he may serve a Declaration on the Tenant in Possession or fix it upon any notorious Part of the Premises and may Recover back his Term; but it is recoverable by the Tenant if within Six Months he pays his Rent and all Costs & Charges in the Action—

The Plaintiff in this Action must make Affidavit of the Rent due, & that there was not Sufficient Distress & that he had the Right of Entry &C.—

The Books are positive in requiring great particularity in discribing the premises with Certainty & the Different Parcels & kinds of Land that the Sheriff may know to deliver the Possession with certainty; but this seems   for in Fact it is said you are not bound to lay the real quantity of each but a feigned Quantity; & there are Authentic Precedents which do not enter into such Details & where it is only said, a Messuage with the Appurtenances in D. It is held assential [174] among our Practitioners to peculiarize, also it is the present Practice for the Sheriff to deliver you

---

[158] An Act for the more effectual securing the Payment of Rents, and preventing Frauds by Tenants, 11 Geo 2, c. 19, sec. 12 (1738).

Possession of as much as you Claim, on your giving him security to indamnify him for the Consequence.—

If there are several Parcels in the hands of several Persons, there must be as many Deliveries of Possession. If the Sheriff delivers Possession to the Lessor, and the Defendant ousts him, besides the Method of gaining Possession by *an alias Habere Facias Possessionem* (to the Lessor upon Affidavit)[159] in case the first was not absolutely returned, the Lessor upon Affidavit of the Fact may have an Attachment against the Defendant to punish him for his Contempt of the Court.—

When an Infant brings an Ejectment there must be two Demises laid in the Declaration, the first from the Infant & the second from the Guardian or next Friend prosecuting for the Infant. It is Observed in the Books of Practice, that the Lease set forth in the Decla[ra]tion in Cases where an Infant is Lessor must always be in Consideration of Rent reserved, however in a Case reported by *Burrows*,[160] Question "how far the Acts of an Infant are void [175] or voidable," the Reservation of Rent is laid down as not necessary; this is a most important Case.—

If the Lessor be put in Possession, and be Immediately turned out by a Stranger the Party's only Remedy is by the Statutes of *Forcible Entry & Detainer*,[161] or bringing an other Ejectment, for the Law presumes the Stranger claims under a Title established by the Trial.

The Law is different where the Stranger disturbs the Sheriff in the Act of delivering Possession, for here it stands on the same footing with any Mans disturbing the Execution of Legal Process, & an Attachment may be had against him.—

If you want to bring an Action of Ejectment for several, & are in Doubt whether they ought to Obtain as Coparceners, Joint Tenants or Tenants in

---

[159] The words *to the Lessor upon Affidavit* are underscored and overscored in the original manuscript, seemingly indicating a question about the use of the phrase. This same sentence without the indicated phrase is found in Wyche, *NY Supreme Court Practice* (2d ed. 1794) 270. Similar scoring is at p. [8], *supra*. See n. 14, *supra*.

[160] Zouch, *ex dimiss*. Abbot & Hallet v. Parsons, 3 Burr. 1794 (KB 1765). The correct quotation of the question posed by the case is "Whether an Infant's Conveyance by Lease and Release was absolutely VOID, or only VOIDABLE." *Ibid*.

[161] Forcible Entries, 5 Rich 2 Stat 1, c. 7 (1381); 15 Rich 2, c. 2 (1391); 4 Hen 4, c. 8 (1402); 8 Hen 6, c. 9 (1429); 31 Eliz 1, c. 11 (1588).

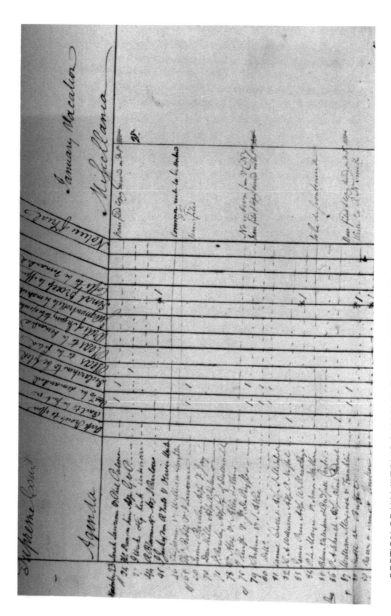

PORTION OF HAMILTON'S SUPREME COURT AGENDA FOR JANUARY VACATION, 1786

Courtesy Library of Congress

common, the best Way is to lay several Demises, & conclude with a Joint Demise; this Precaution will cover any Title that will unfold itself on the Trial or Question tho' simple, is generally made one of the bugbear Questions on an Examination.—

It was Delivered by Lord Mansfield in delivering the Oppinion of the Court in a [176] Case of Trespass[162] for mesne Profits, that the bare Production of the Record of Recovery in Ejectment is a Sufficient Proof of the Plaintiffs Title, whether the Plaintiff be Lessor or Lessee or whether the Tenant was made Defendant or suffered Judgment by Default; this however is applicable to the Time of the Demise laid in the Declaration of Ejectment; for if the Time of Enjoying the mesne Profits laid in the Declaration in Trespass exceeds the Demise in the Declaration of Ejectment, the Plaintiff must prove his Title during the Time beyond the Demise, by Evidence dehors the Record of Recovery. From this Doctrine results the necessity of making your Term in your Declaration of Ejectment large enough to comprehend your Claim to the mesne Profits.—

The Plaintiff must be careful after Issue Joined how he enters into the Premisses, for if he enters into any Part it may be pleaded in abatement of the Action by Plea, *puis darein continuance.*—

It is in the Breast of the Judge of *nisi prius* [177] whether he will accept of such Plea, or not (i.e.) whether he will or will not proceed in the Trial. The Party ought to make it appear that it is a True Plea.—

If the Judge Receives the Plea it stops the Trial, and the Plaintiff is not to reply to it at the Assizes, but the Judge is to return it as Parcel of the Record of *Nisi prius.* Yele. 180. Cro. Car. 261.—[163]

---

[162] Aslin v. Parker, 2 Burr. 665, 32 Geo 2 (KB 1758).
[163] Moore v. Hawkins, Yelv. 180 (KB 1611).

PRACTICE
AND PROCEDURE

EXHIBITS

A-1. Bill of Middlesex

King's Bench, England, 1771
[3 Blackstone, *Commentaries* xviii]

Middlesex, to wit } *The Sheriff* is commanded that he take Charles Long, late of Burford, in the county of Oxford, if he may be found in his bailiwick, and him safely keep, so that he may have his body before the lord the king at Westminster, on . . . to answer William Burton, gentleman, of a plea of trespass; (*and also* to a bill of the said William against the aforesaid Charles, for two hundred pounds of debt, according to the custom of the court of the said lord the king, before the king himself to be exhibited;) and that he have there then this precept.

◆ ◆ ◆

A-2. Bill of Albany

Supreme Court, New York State, 1793
[Misc. Mss. HR]

[Seal]   It is Commanded the Sheriff that he take William Bott if he shall be found within his Bailiwick and him safely keep so that he may have his Body before us at the City Hall of the City of Albany on Saturday the Twenty Sixth day of October Instant to answer John Hoffnagle Administrator of all and singular the Goods and Chattles Rights and Credits of Melchor Hoffnagle Deceased of a plea of Trespass and also to a Bill of the said John administrator as aforesaid against the said William for Four Hundred Pounds upon Promises according to the Custom of our Court before us to be exhibited. And have then there this Precept

Ten Broeck Atty

By Bill
McKesson

◆ ◆ ◆

B-1. CAPIAS

Common Pleas, England, 1766
[1 Richardson, *Common Pleas Practice* (4th ed. 1769) 74-75]

[Seal]   GEORGE the third, &c. To the sheriff of *Middlesex*, greeting.
                We command you, that you take J.B. late of the parish of *St.
Clement Danes* in your county, *Taylor*, if he shall be found in your bailiwic, and
keep him safely, so that you may have his body before our justices at
Westminster on the octave of *St. Hilary*, to answer W.P. in a plea, wherefore with
force and arms he broke the *Close* of the said *W.* at Westminster, and did other
injuries to him, to his great damage, and against our peace; and have there this
writ. Witness *Sir John Eardley Wilmot*, knight, at *Westminster*, the twenty-ninth
day of *November* in the seventh year of our reign.

◆ ◆ ◆

B-2. CAPIAS

Supreme Court, New York Colony, c. 1760
[Livingston, *Ms. Precedent Book* 31]

[Seal]   GEORGE THE THIRD by the Grace of God of Great Brittain
                France and Ireland King Defender of the Faith &c. To our
Sheriff of _____ County GREETING We Command you that you take A. B. if
he shall be found within your Bailiwick and him safely keep so that you have
his Body before us at the City of *New York* on the third Tuesday of _____ next
(the day on which the writ is returnable) to answer C.D. of a Plea of Trespass
&c. And have you then there this Writ Witness James DeLancey Esqr. Chief
Justice of our Province of New York at New York the _____ Day of _____ (the
last Day of the preceeding Term) in the _____ year of our Reign—

Livingston Attorney—   Clarke Junr.

◆ ◆ ◆

B-3. CAPIAS

Supreme Court, New York State, 1797
[Misc. Ms. HR]

[Seal]   The People of the State of New York by the Grace of God free and independent to the Sheriff of the City & County of New York greeting We command you that you take Tredwell Jackson if he shall be found within your bailiwick and him safely keep so that you may have his body before us in our Supreme Court at the City of New York on the last tuesday of July next to answer unto Nathaniel Gardiner Jonathan Thompson and Cornelius White of a plea of trespass and have you then there this writ Witness Robert Yates Esquire Chief Justice at Albany the twenty ninth day of April in the twenty first year of our Independence—

Hamilton Atty   Fairlie

C. LATITAT

Supreme Court, New York State, 1793
[Wyche, *NY Supreme Court Practice* (2d ed. 1794) 44]

[Seal]   The people of the state of New-York, by the grace of God, free and independent: to the sheriff of our county of *Orange*, greeting: whereas we lately commanded our sheriff of *Albany*, that he should take *Benjamin Bell*, if he should be found in his bailiwick, and him safely keep, so that he might have his body before us, at our city of *Albany*, at a certain day now past, to answer *Abraham Adams*, of a plea of trespass; and our said sheriff of *Albany* at that day returned to us, that the said *Benjamin* was not found in his bailiwick; whereupon, on the behalf of the aforesaid *Abraham*, it is sufficiently testified in our court, before us, that the said *Benjamin* doth lurk up and down and secrete himself in your county; therefore, we command you, that you take him, if he shall be found in your bailiwick, and him safely keep, so that you may have his body before us, at our city of *Albany*, on *the third Tuesday of October next*, to answer the said *Abraham*, of the plea *and bill* aforesaid; and have you then there this writ. Witness *Robert Yates*, esq; chief justice, at our city of *Albany*, the *eleventh* day of *August*, in the *seventeenth* year of our independence.

C. *Clark*, attorney.   *M'Kesson*.

◆ ◆ ◆

D. Venire

Supreme Court, New York State, 1799
[Misc. Mss. HR]

[Seal]   The People of the State of New York by the Grace of God Free and Independent To the Sheriff of the City and County of New York Greeting We Command you that you cause to come before our Justices of our Supreme Court of Judicature at the City Hall of the City of Albany on the third Tuesday of January next (or before our Chief Justice or other Justice or Justices of our Said Supreme Court or Some or one of them if before that day to wit on the twelfth day of November next at the City Hall of the City of New York at a Circuit Court for the trial of Issues Joined or to be—Joined in Our Said Supreme Court or in Any other Court and brought into the Said Supreme Court to be tried and which are or may be triable at Said City of New York they any or either of them According to the form of the Act—in Such Case made and Provided Shall Come) twelve free and—and Lawful men of your City and County each of whom Shall have in his Own Name or right or in trust for him or in his wife's right a Freehold in lands Messuages or tenements or a Personal Estate of the Value of Sixty Pounds free of All reprises debts demands or Encomberances Whatsoever by whom the truth of the matter may be better known and who neither Frederick Jay Plaintiff nor James Rivington and James Rivington the younger Defendants in any affinity do touch to enquire into the truth of all and every of Certain Breaches of Covenant by the Said James Rivington and James

Rivington the younger as the Said Frederick Jay hath in our Supreme Court above suggested on [   ] and to Assess the damages that the Said Frederick Jay hath sustained thereby and we do further Command our Said Justices or Such of them who shall hold the Said Circuit Court to make return thereof to our Said Supreme Court at the City Hall of the City of Albany on the third Tuesday of January next and have you then these the Names of the Jurors and this writ Witness John Lansing Junior Esquire Chief Justice at our City of Albany the twenty Sixth day of October in the twenty fourth year of Our Independence.

Hamilton Atty   Bloodgood Clk

E. DISTRINGAS

Printed Form, Supreme Court, New York State, 1798
[Misc. Mss. HR]

THE PEOPLE of the State of New York, by the GRACE of GOD, Free and
Independent, To the Sheriff of the *City and* County of
[Seal]   *New York* Greeting: WE command you that you distrain
the bodies of the several persons named in the pannel here-
unto annexed, Jurors summoned in our Supreme Court of Judicature for the said State, before our Justices of our said Court, between *John Rathbone* the Plaintiff and *Abraham J. Adriance* the Defendant by all their Lands and Chattels in your bailiwick, so that neither they, nor any one of them, do inter-meddle therewith, until you have further command from us in that behalf, and that you answer unto us for the issues of the same so that you have the bodies of the said Jurors before our Justices of our said Supreme Court of Judicature at the City-Hall of the city of *New York* on the *last* Tuesday of *July* next, or before the Chief Justice, or other Justices or Justice of the said Supreme Court, or some or one of them, if before that day, to wit, on *Thursday* the *nineteenth* day of *July next at the City Hall of the City of New York* at a Circuit Court for the trial of all issues, joined or to be joined in the said Supreme

Court, or in any other Court, and brought into the said Supreme Court to be tried, and which are or may be triable in the said *City and* County of *New York* they or either of them, according to the form of the Statute in such case made and provided, shall come to make a certain Jury of the country between the parties aforesaid, of a plea of *Trespass on the case* and to hear their judgment for their former defaults. And have you then there the names of those Jurors, and this writ. WITNESS, JOHN LANSING, Junior, Esquire, Chief Justice at the City of *Albany* the *twenty eighth* day of *April* and in the *twenty second* year of our Independence.

Rose Atty   Fairlie and Bloodgood

———————◆ ◆ ◆———————

F. PORTION OF ISSUE ROLL

Including Award of Venire and Respiting of Jury

Supreme Court, New York State, 1784
[Jackson ex dem. Leonard v. Post, Parchment Roll (HR)]

Therefore let a Jury come thereupon before the People of the State of New York in their Supreme Court of Judicature on the third tuesday of October next wheresoever the said Court shall thus be holden in the State aforesaid who neither &c. to recognise &c. because as well &c. The same day is there given to the parties aforesaid.—

Pleas before the People of the State of New York at the City of Albany of the term of October in the Ninth Year of the Independence of the said State and in the Year of our Lord One thousand seven hundred and Eighty four. Witness Richard Morris Esquire Chief Justice.

Roll   McKesson

New York to wit. The Jury between James Jackson Plaintiff and Anthony Post Defendant of a plea of Trespass and ejectment of farm is respited before the people of the State of New York in their Supreme Court of Judicature until the third tuesday of January next; unless the Chief Justice or other Justice or Justices of the said People at a Court for trial of causes arising in the County aforesaid brought to issue in the said Supreme Court shall first come on Tuesday the twenty first Day of December next at the City Hall of the said City in the County aforesaid according to the form of the Ordinance and Act in that case made and provided for default of Jurors because none of them did appear.

Therefore let the Sheriff have the Bodies of the said Jurors to make the said Jury between the parties aforesaid at the same place.

And be it known that the Writ of the said People in this Case upon record was delivered to the Sheriff of the County aforesaid the thirty first day of October in this same term before the People of the State of New York at the City of Albany to be executed according to law at his peril.—

New York ss. Nisi Prius between James Jackson Plaintiff and Anthony Post Defendant of a Plea of Trespass and Ejectment of farm &c. returnable at the City of New York, in the County of N Yk on the twenty first day of December in the Year of our Lord one thousand seven hundred and Eighty four—

    Hamilton attorney—   McKesson

G. Subpoena

Supreme Court, New York State, 1786
[Clinton, *Ms. Precedent Book* 21]

The People of the State of New York by the Grace of God free and independent To Thomas White Greeting; We command you and each of you firmly injoining that all and singular your business and excuses whatsoever ceasing in your proper persons you and each of you be before our Justices of our Supreme Court some or one of them on Tuesday the twenty eighth day of November instant at the City Hall of the City of New York To testify all and singular what you or either of you know in a certain cause in our Court before us now depending and undetermined between William Wynbrook Plaintiff and Daniel Delavan Defendant in a plea of Debt on the part of the Plaintiff and at that day by a Jury of the Country to be tried and this do you nor either of you in any wise omit under the penalty upon each of you one hundred pounds; Witness Richard Morris Esquire Chief Justice at New York the twefth day of September in the eleventh Year of our Independence—

B. Atty   Mc Kesson

H. Bail Piece

Supreme Court, New York State, 1797
[Misc. Mss. HR]

Supreme   Of the Term of October in the year of our lord one
Court   thousand seven hundred and ninety six—

City and County of New York ss—Joseph Lindley and Richard Hartshorne who are impleaded with Frederick Rhinelander William Rhinelander Philip Rhinelander and William Kenyan are Delivered to Bail on a Cepi Corpus to

Peter Elting—of the second ward of the City of New York Merchant and John Doe of the same place Gentleman—

> At the suit of Saturnine
> Bernard Garrick and Cornelius
> Christian Westfall in a plea of
> Trespass on the Case—

> A. Hamilton Atty

Taken and acknowledged
the 13th day of January
MDCCXCVII *Morn. Lewis*

I. Bail Bond

Printed Form, Supreme Court, New York State, 1788
[Ewart v. Coulthard (Ms. HR)]

Know all Men by these Presents, that we *William Kelly and John Billings* are held and firmly bound unto Herman Hoffman, Esquire, Sheriff of the County of Dutchess, in the Sum of *Two Hundred and Eighty Pounds*—Lawful Money of the State of New York, to be paid to the said Herman Hoffman, or his certain Attorney, Executors, Administrators or Assigns; to which payment well and truly to be made, we bind ourselves, and each of us, jointly and severally, our, and each of our Heirs, Executors and Administrators, firmly by these Presents. Sealed with our Seals, dated this *Second* Day of *January* in the Year of our Lord, One thousand Seven Hundred and Eighty *Eight.*

The Condition of this Obligation is such, That if the above bounden *William Kelly* shall personally appear before *us at the City of New York on the Third Tuesday in January Next to answer unto James Pine Administrator of All and Singular the Goods and Chattels and Credits which were of James Pine Deceased, with the will annexed of the Said James Pine of a Plea of Trespass and also to the Bill of the said James Against the Said William for one Hundred and forty Pounds of Debt According to the Custom of our Court Before us to be exhibited.* Then the above Obligation to be void and of no effect, otherwise to remain in full Force and Virtue.

<table>
<tr><td>Sealed and Delivered
in the Presence of }</td><td style="text-align:center">his
William X Kelly (LS)
mark</td></tr>
<tr><td>Peter V D Burgh</td><td>John Billings (LS)</td></tr>
</table>

———◆ ◆ ◆———

J. Assignment of Bail Bond

Printed Form, Supreme Court, New York State, 1788
[Ewart v. Coulthard (Ms. HR)]
[Endorsement of Bail Bond]

I, Herman Hoffman, Esq; Sheriff of Dutchess County, do hereby assign the within written Bail Bond, to the Use of the Plaintiff, to be sued for by *him* according to the Form and Effect of the Statute, in that Case made and provided
In Witness Whereof, I have hereunto set my Hand and Seal of my office, this *first* Day of *March* in the Year of our Lord, One Thousand Seven Hundred and Eighty *Eight*.

<table>
<tr><td>Sealed and Delivered }
in the Presence of</td><td>Herman Hoffman (LS)</td></tr>
<tr><td>Peter V D. Burgh
John Lloyd</td><td></td></tr>
</table>

———◆ ◆ ◆———

K. Supersedeas

Supreme Court, New York State, 1808

[Caines, *Forms* 121]

The People of the State of *New-York*, &c. To the sheriff of   ,
GREETING: Whereas by our writ we lately commanded you, that you should
take C. D. if he should be found in your bailiwick, and him safely keep, so that
you might have his body before our justices of our supreme court of judicature, at the city-hall of the city of *New-York*, on the first Monday of *May* then
next, to answer A. B. of a plea of trespass, and also to a bill of the said A. B.
to be exhibited against the said C. D. for   dollars upon promises, (or
as the plea is) according to the custom of our court before our said justices in
our court aforesaid: And because the said A. B. hath not declared against the
said C. D. within two terms next after the return of the said writ, and the said
C. D. hath come into our said court before our justices thereof, and filed common bail at the suit of the said A. B. in the plea and to the bill aforesaid; therefore we command you, that you wholly cease from taking, attaching, impris-
oning, or in any wise molesting the said C. D. on the occasion aforesaid; and
if you have taken the said C. D. and detain him in prison on that occasion, and
no other, that then without delay you cause him to be delivered out of the
prison wherein he is so detained, at your peril. Witness *James Kent*, Esquire,
our Chief-Justice, &c.

L. Attachment of Privilege

Supreme Court, New York State, 1799

[Misc. Mss. CA]

[Seal]   The people of the State of New York. To the Sheriff of
               Montgomery greeting. We command you that you Attach
Asa Wade if he may be found in your bailiwick & him safely keep so that you
may have his body before our Justices of our Supreme Court of Judicature at

the City Hall at the City of New York on the last Tuesday of July next to answer James Emott Gentleman one of the attornies of our Court before our said Justices according to the liberties and priviledges of such Attornies & other ministers of the same Court from time whereof the memory of man is not to the Contrary used & approved of in the same Court of a plea of Trespass And also to a bill of the said James against the said Asa for a debt of fifty three Dollars & sixty seven Cents according to the custom of our said Court before our said Justices to be then & there exhibited—And have you there then this Writ—Witness John Lansing Junior Esquire Chief Justice at the City of New York the twentysixth day of April in the twentyfourth year of our Independence.

           Cook Atty   Bloodgood Clk

———————◆ ◆ ◆———————

M. PLEA TO THE GENERAL ISSUE IN TRESPASS

New York Mayor's Court, 1786
[Hamilton Papers (Ms. LC)]

New York Mayor's Court

George Stanton
      ads.   }
Thomas Ivers Esquire

           And the said George by Alexander Hamilton his Attorney comes and defends the force and Injury when &c. and says that he is not guilty thereof; and of this he puts himself upon the Country and the said Thomas in like manner &c

                        Hamilton for the defendt.

City of New York ss George Stanton puts in his place Alexander Hamilton his Attorney at the suit of Thomas Ivers Esquire in the Plea aforesaid

———————◆ ◆ ◆———————

N. Plea of Non Est Factum

New York Mayor's Court, 1786
[A. J. Marino, Weehawken, N.J.]

New York Mayor's Court

Benjamin Palmer
& Joseph Mullinex } Plea
ads.
William Rodman

    And the said Benjamin and Joseph by Alexander Hamilton their Attorney come and defend the force and injury when &c. and say, that they ought not to be charged with the said debt, by means of the said writing obligatory, because they say that the said writing obligatory is not their deed; and of this they put themselves upon the Country and the said William in like manner &c.

            Hamilton Atty. for the defts.

City of New York ss. Benjamin Palmer and Joseph Mullinex put in their place Alexander Hamilton their Attorney at the suit of William Rodman in the plea aforesaid

O. Plea of Nil Debet

New York Mayor's Court, c. 1785
[Hamilton Papers (Ms. LC)]

Mayors Court

Thomas Pearsall
    ads.   }   Plea
Oliver Arnold

       And the said Thomas by Brockholst Livingston his Attorney comes and defends the force and injury when &c and says that he does not owe to the said Oliver the said seventy seven pounds nineteen shillings and seven pence nor any part thereof in manner and form as the said declaration complains against him and of this he puts himself upon the Country & the said Oliver doth the like &c.

                    B. Livingston atty for deft

City of New York ss Thomas Pearsall puts in his place Brockholst Livingston his Attorney at the suit of Oliver Arnold in the Plea aforesaid

P. Plea of Non Assumpsit

Supreme Court, New York State
[Hamilton Papers (Ms. LC)]

Supreme Court

who is implead with
  Benjamin Mgnac
John Magnac ^
    adsm
Peter Buchey
}

       And the said John who is impleaded with the said Benjamin by Alexander Hamilton his Attorney comes and defends the Wrong and Injury when &c. and says that he together with the said Benjamin did not undertake and promise in manner and form as the aforesaid Peter above complains against them and of this he puts himself upon the country and the aforesaid Peter doth the like &c.

                       A. Hamilton for ~~Plf~~ Deft
                       J. Morton for ~~Deft~~ Plf

City & County of New York, to wit, John Mgnac who is impleaded with Benjamin Magnac puts in his place Alexander Hamilton his Attorney at the suit of ~~against~~ Peter Buchey in the plea aforesaid—

Q. WRIT OF DOWER

Printed Form, Supreme Court, New York State, 1799
[Misc. Mss. CA]

[Seal]   The People of the State of New-York to the Sheriff of the County of *Orange*—Greeting Command *Robert McNeely* that justly and without delay he render unto *Sarah McNeely* widow who was the wife of *Henry McNeely* her reasonable dower which falleth to her out of the Freehold which was of the said *Henry McNeely* heretofore husband in *the town of New Windsor* in the county of *Orange* aforesaid whereof she nothing hath as she says and of which she complains that the aforesaid *Robert McNeely* hath deforced her and unless he shall so do and the aforesaid *Sarah McNeely* shall give you sufficient security for prosecuting her claim then summon the aforesaid *Robert McNeely* by good summoners that he be before *our* Justices of our Supreme Court of judicature at the *city hall of the* city of *Albany* on *the third tuesday of January next* there to shew why he hath not so done and have then there those summoners and this Writ Witness *Robert R. Livingston Esq* our Chancellor at *the City of New York* the *fourteenth day of December* in the *twenty fourth* Year of our Independence 1799.

Bowman Atty   *Kip Clk*

◆ ◆ ◆

R. WRIT OF REPLEVIN

Supreme Court, New York State, 1803
[Misc. Mss. CA]

[Seal]   The People of the State of New York by the Grace of Go[d] free and Independent   To the Sheriff of the County of Greene Greeting. if Samuel Hemenway of the Town of Freehold, in the County of Green, Carpenter, shall give you security, to prosecute his complaint and to return two Scythes one Snathe and tacklin [listing many farm and personal possessions], five Dollars Specie which Nathan Bruce of the Town of Cocksakie, in the County of Green aforesaid Yeoman, Took and unjustly detains against gages and pledges, as he saith, if return, thereof shall be adjudged; then cause the aforesaid Goods and Chattels, to be replevied and delivered to the aforesaid Samuel Hemenway, without delay, and Summon by good Summoners, the aforesaid Nathan Bruce, that he be before our Justices of our Supreme Court of Judicature of the State of New York at the City Hall of the City of New York on the second Monday of November next to answer the aforesaid Samuel Hemenway of a plea of taking and unjustly detaining the Goods and Chattles aforesaid and have you then there this Writ Witness John Lansing Junior Esquire Chancellor of said State at the City of Albany the twenty seventh day of September in the twenty eight year of our Independence.

H. Burham, Atty—   Richard S. Treat   Clk in Chy

S. ELEGIT

King's Bench, England, 1776

[1 Richardson, *Attorney's Practice* (6th ed. 1776) 364-365]

GEORGE the third, by the grace of God, of *Great Britain, France* and *Ireland*, king, defender of the faith, &c. To the sheriff of *Essex* greeting: Whereas R. R. esq; lately in our court before us at *Westminster*, by bill without our writ, and by the judgment of the same court, recovered against W. S. gent, otherwise called, &c. one thousand pounds of debt, and also fifteen pounds for his damages which he has sustained, as well by occasion of the detaining that debt, as for his costs and charges by him about his suit in that behalf expended, whereof the said W. S. is convicted, as appears to us of record; and whereupon in our same court before us, it is considered that the said R. R. have his execution against F. W. C. B. and E. G. tenants of one messuage, five barns, and two stables, one garden, one orchard, twenty acres of land, and twenty acres of meadow, fifty acres of pasture, and ten acres of wood, with the appurtenances, situate, lying and being in the parish of *Westham* in your county, which were the lands and tenements of the said *W. S.* deceased, (of which the said *W. S.* on the day of giving the said judgment, and afterwards was seised in his demesne as of fee) of the debt and damages aforesaid to be levied of those lands and tenements; and afterwards the said *R. R.* came in our said court before us, and, according to the form of the statute in such case made and provided, chose a moiety of the said lands and tenements to be delivered to him by a reasonable price and extent, to hold to him and his assigns as his free tenement, according to the form of the said statute, until the said debt and damages shall be thereof fully levied: we therefore command you, that without delay you cause a moiety of all the said lands and tenements to be delivered to the said *R. R.* by a reasonable price and extent, to hold to him and his assigns as a free tenement, according to the form of the said statute, until the said debt and damages shall be thereof fully levied; and in what manner you shall execute this our precept, make appear to us at *Westminster*, on   next after   remitting to us this our writ. Witness, *&c:*

◆ ◆ ◆

T. Capias Ad Satisfaciendum
Supreme Court, New York State, 1786
[Clinton, *Ms. Precedent Book* 23-24]

[Seal]   The People of the State of New York by the Grace of God free and independent to the Sheriff of our County of Orange Greeting We command you that you take Thomas Horton if he shall be found within your Bailiwick and him safely keep so that you may have his body before us at Albany on the third tuesday in October next to satisfy unto William Fraeger of one hundred pounds Current Money of New York which he the said William hath recovered before us and also eight pounds 16/3 which to the said William in our same Court before us were adjudged for his damages which he hath sustained as well by occasion of detaining that debt as for his costs & Charges by him about his suit in that behalf expended whereof the said Thomas is convicted as appears to us of Record and have then there this Writ   Witness Richard Morris Esquire Chief Justice at Albany the fifth day of August in the eleventh year of our Independence.

Ogilvie   McKesson

— ◆ ◆ ◆ —

U. Testatum Fieri Facias

Supreme Court, New York State, 1798
[Prior v. Morehouse, NY Supreme Court, 1798 (Ms. CA)]

[Seal]   The People of the State of New York by the grace of God free Independent; To our Sheriff of our County of Rensselaer, greeting: Whereas we lately commanded our Sheriff of our County of Washington, that of the Goods and Chattels of Abraham Morehouse, otherwise called Abraham Morehouse of Johnstown, in the County of Montgomery, in the State of New York, in his [B]ailiwick, he should cause to be made Forty Thousand Dollars of Debt, which Edmund Prior lately in our Supreme Court of Judicature, before us at New York, recovered against him, and also fifteen Dollars, forty four Cents, which in our same Court, to the same Edmund were adjudged for his damages which he had sustained as well by occasion of the detention of that debt, as for his Costs and Charges by him about his suit in that behalf expended: whereof the said Abraham Morehouse is convicted as it appears to us of Record: and if sufficient goods and Chattels of the said Abraham Morehouse could not be found in his Bailiwick, that then he should cause the Debt, damages and Costs aforesaid, to be made of the Lands and Tenements whereof the said Abraham Morehouse was seized on the nineteenth day of January, in the year of our Lord one thousand seven hundred and ninety seven, or at anytime afterwards, in whose hands soever the same might be: And that he should have those monies before our Justices of our Supreme Court of Judicature, at the City of Albany on the Third Tuesday of January now instant, to render unto the said Edmund Prior for his Debt and Damages aforesaid: And our said Sheriff of Washington on that day returned to our Justices of our same Court, that by virtue of that writ to him directed, he had caused to be made of the lands and Tenements of the [sa]id Abraham Ten Thousand Dollars, parcel of the Debt and Damages aforesaid, which said money he had ready before Justices of our Same Court at the day & place aforesaid, as by that writ he was commanded; and that he the said Abraham Morehouse had no goods and Chattels, nor had he any other or more lands and Tenements in his Bailiwick, whereof he would cause to be made the residue of the Debt and damages aforesaid: And now on the behalf of the said Edmund Prior in our said Court before our Justices of the same Court it is sufficiently testified that the said Abraham Morehouse hath sufficient goods and Chattels Lands and Tenements in your Bailiwick to satisfy the said Edmund the residue of the Debt and Damages aforesaid: Therefore we command you, that of the goods and Chattels of the said Abraham in your Bailiwick you cause to be made Thirty Thousand and fifteen Dollars forty four Cents, residue of the Debt and Damages aforesaid: and if sufficient goods and Chattels of the said Abraham can not be found in your Bailiwick, that then you cause the said Thirty Thousand & Fifteen Dollars & forty four Cents residue of the Debt and Damages aforesaid to be made of the Lands and Tenements in your Bailiwick, whereof the said Abraham Morehouse was seized on the said nineteenth day of January in the year of our Lord one thousand seven hundred and ninety seven, or at any time afterwards in whose hands soever the same may be, and that you have that money before our Justice of our Supreme Court of Judicature aforesaid at the City Hall of the City of Albany on the Third Tuesday of April next to be paid to the said Edmund for the residue of the debt and Damages aforesaid; And have there then this writ: Witness Robert Yates Esquire Chief Justice at the City of Albany the twenty seventh day of January in the year of our Lord one thousand seven hundred and ninety eight and of our Independence the twenty Second—

Hamilton   Bloodgood Clerk

V. PLURIES TESTATUM CAPIAS AD SATISFACIENDUM

Supreme Court, New York State, 1798
[Bryson v. Goodrich, NY Supreme Court, 1798 (Ms. CA)]

[Seal]   The People of the State of New York by the Grace of God free and Independent to the Sheriff of the County of Columbia Greeting Whereas we lately commanded the Sheriff of our City and County of New York that he should take Elihu Chauncey Goodrich otherwise called Elihu Chauncey Goodrich Gentlemen one of the Attornies of our Supreme Court of Judicature if he should be found in [h]is [Baili]wick and him safely keep so that he might have his body before us in our Supreme Court to satisfy James Bryson of one thousand two hundred and twenty pounds one shilling and two pence amounting to three thousand and fifty Dollars and fourteen Cents which the said James Bryson lately in our said Court before us at Albany recovered against the said Elihu Chauncey Goodrich for his Damages which he had sustained as well by occasion of the not performing certain promises and undertakings lately made by the said Elihu Chauncey Goodrich to the said James Bryson as for his Costs and Charges by him about his suit in that behalf expended whereof the said Elihu Chauncey Goodrich was convicted as appears to us of record and the said Sheriff hath thereon returned to us that the said Elihu Chauncey Goodrich is not found in his Bailiwick upon which on the part of the said James Bryson in our Supreme Court before us at New York it is sufficiently testified that the said Elihu Chauncey Goodrich runs up and down and secretes himself in your County Therefore we command you as oftentimes we have commanded you that you take him if he shall be found within your Bailiwick and him safely keep so that you may have his body before our Justices of our Supreme Court of Judicature at the City of Albany on the third Tuesday of April next to satisfy the said James Bryson the Damages aforesaid and have you then there this writ Witness Robert Yates Esquire Chief Justice at Albany the sixteenth day of January in the twenty second year of our Independence—

Hamilton Atty   Fairlie

W. Habere Facias Possessionem
Supreme Court, New York State, 1808
[Caines, *Forms* 484]

The People of the State of *New-York,* &c. to the sheriff of   , GREETING: Whereas *John Doe* lately in our supreme court of judicature, before our justices of the same court, at the city-hall of the city of   , by our writ, (or if by *bill,* say "by bill without our writ,") and by the judgment of the same court, recovered against C. D.* his term then and yet to come of and in   dwelling-houses, &c. (as in the declaration in ejectment,) with the appurtenances, situate and being in the parish of   , in your county, which A. B. on the   day of   , in the year of our Lord one thousand eight hundred and   , had demised to the said *John Doe,* to hold the same to the said John Doe and his assigns, from the   day of   then last past, for and during and unto the full end and term of   years from thence next ensuing, and fully to be complete and ended; by virtue of which said demise, the said *John Doe* entered into the said tenements with the appurtenances, and was possessed thereof, until the said C. D. afterwards, to wit, on the   day of   , in the year aforesaid, with force and arms, &c. entered into the said tenements with the appurtenances, which the said A. B. had demised to the said *John Doe,* in manner and for the term aforesaid, which was not then nor is yet expired, and ejected the said *John Doe* from his said farm; whereof the said C. D. is convicted, as appears to us of record: Therefore we command you, that without delay you cause the said *John Doe* to have the possession of his said term yet to come of and in the tenements aforesaid with the appurtenances; and in what manner you shall have executed this our writ, make appear to our said justices, at the city-hall of the city of   , on the Monday of   next, &c.

---

* If the judgment was by default, the execution is against *Richard Roe,* the casual ejector.

X. BILL OF COSTS

Supreme Court, New York State, 1789
[The Johns Hopkins University Library (Ms.)]

New York Supreme Court

William Davenport ⎫
     vs.   ⎬   Costs
<u>Thomas Thomas</u> ⎭

Octr. Novr. 1786

Retaining fee warrant of Attorney and filing	£1-12-3	
Latitat fol 4. engrossing and seal	<u>12-3</u>	
		2-4-6

January term 1787		
Sheriff's fees	12-6	
filing writ	1-0	
motion and rule for body	6-6	
Motion and rule to plead	6-6	
Judges fee	5-0	
Cryer and bellringer	1-9	
Term fee	<u>5-0</u>	
		2-8-3

April term fee	<u>5-0</u>	
		5-0

April Vacation		
drawing Narr. fol. 7 @ 1/6	10-6	
Copy to file and filing	7-0	
copy of plea fol. 3	1-6	
drawing issue Roll fol 14	1- 1-0	
Engrossing inde	14-0	
filing	1-0	
July term fee	<u>5-0</u>	
		3-0-0

January term 1788		
drawing Venire fol 4. engrossing and Seal ..	12-3	
Return and filing	<u>9-0</u>	
		1-1-3

January Vacation

Entering 3 continuances on the roll	4-6
drawing nisi prius record fol 15. @ 1/6	1- 2-6
Engrossing inde and Seal	17-3
Brief for trial and copy	9-0
drg. notice of trial copy and service	4-0
drg. abstract of pleadings fol 1-@ 1/6	1-6
two copies thereof @ 6∂	1-0
serving one copy on Judge	1-6
Do. on Clerk	1-6
Drg. distringas fol 5 engrossing & Seal	14-9
Drg. Subpoena fol 4 engrossing and Seal ...	12-3
Drawing Ticket fol 3-@ 1/6	4-6
4 Copies	6-0
motion that nisi prius record be received and cause made a remanet	5-0
motion that sheriff return Venire & distringas	5-0
Sheriff for returning Venire & distringas ...	2-0
Atty. & Counsel's trial fee being prepared ..	2- 2-0
motion and rule for discontinuance	6-6
drawing costs and copy	3-0
Serving Subpoena	4-0
gave witnesses	4-0
4 witnesses attending 8 days from foreign county	7- 4-0

		15-15-9
Carried over		£24-14-9
brought over		£24-14-9
drg. affidavit of witnesses fol 10 @ 1/6	£0-15-0	
Copy thereof @ 6∂	5-0	
Judge for Oath	1-0	
Clerk of Circuits fees	5- 4-0	
		6- 5-0
		£30-19-9

New York March 9th. 1789 Received from Aaron Burr Esquire the amount of the foregoing bill of Costs—

Alexander Hamilton

Y. SCIRE FACIAS

Supreme Court, New York State, 1795

[Misc. Ms. HR]

[Seal]   The People of the State of New York by the grace of God free & Independent to the Sheriff of Albany Greeting— Whereas John Roseboom lately in our Court before us at Albany—by bill without our writ and by the Judgment of the same Court recovered against John Harper eight hundred and fifty three pounds for a debt; and also ten pounds thirteen shillings & three pence for his damages which he sustained as well by occasion of the detaining that debt as for his costs & charges by him about his suit in that behalf expended whereof the said John Harper is convicted as appears to us of record. And now on behalf of the said John Roseboom we have been informed that altho' Judgment be thereupon given yet execution for the said debt and damages still remains to be made to him. Whereupon the said John Roseboom hath humbly besought us to provide him a proper remedy in this behalf and we being desirous that what is right and just should be done on this occasion—Command you as we have before commanded you that by good & lawful men of your bailwic you cause it to be made known to the said John Harper that he be before us at the City Hall of the City of New York on the fourth Tuesday of January next to show if he has or knows of anything to say for himself why the said John Roseboom should not have his execution against him for the debt & damages aforesaid, according to the force form and Effect of such recovery, if it shall seem expedient to him so to do. And further to do and receive what our said Court before us shall then & there Consider of him in this behalf. And have you then there the names of those by whom you shall so cause it to be made known to him, together with this writ. Witness Robert Yates Esquire Chief Justice at Albany the fifth—day of November in the twenty first year of our Independence

Van Vechten Atty   Fairlie Clerk

Z. Habeas Corpus Cum Causa

Supreme Court, New York State, 1796
[Misc. Mss. HR]

The People of the State of New York, by the Grace of God, Free and
Independent, To our Mayor, Recorder and Aldermen of
[Seal]   our City of New York; Greeting: We Command You That
you have the Bodies of Abijah Hart and Issac Riley, detained
in our Prison, under your Custody, at the Suit of John Bailey in a Plea of
Trespass on the Case, as it is said, under sure and safe Conduct, together with
the day and Cause of their being detained, by whatsoever Names they shall
be called in the Same. Before our Supreme Court of Judicature, to be holden,
for the said State, at the City of Albany, on the Third Tuesday of October
next, to do and Receive, all and singular those things which our said Court
shall then there, consider of them in this behalf: And have you then there this
Writ; Witness Robert Yates Esquire, Chief Justice at the City of Albany, in
the Twenty first Year of our Independence.—

Wm. Johnson Atty

AA. Procedendo

Supreme Court, New York State, 1795
[Misc. Mss. HR]

[Seal]   The people of the State of New York To the Mayor
Recorder and Aldermen of the City of New York Greeting—
Altho by our writ we lately commanded that the body of Francis Bavetto in
our prison under your Custody as it is said detained under a safe and secure
conduct together with the day and cause of this Caption and detention by
whatever name he might be called in the same you should have before us at
New York on the third tuesday in January instant to do and receive all and

singular those things, which our same Court before us should then and there consider concerning him in that behalf—nevertheless for certain reasons now in our same Court before us especially moving—We command you that in whatever plaints against him at the suit of William G. Miller in our Court before you levied or affirmed and before you now depending undetermined with what speed you can, you—proceed in such manner as according to the law and Custom of this our State of New York you see fit to proceed our writ of Habeas Corpus aforesaid to you before to the contrary thereof directed in any wise not withstanding witness Robert Yates Esquire Chief Justice at New York the thirtieth day of January One thousand sevenhundred and ninety five—

Evertson   Fairlie Clk

BB. Certiorari

Supreme Court, New York State, 1786
[Clinton, *Ms. Precedent Book* 15]

[Seal]   The people of the State of New York by the Grace of God free and independent to Nathaniel Dubon Esquire one of our Justices of the Peace in and for our County of Ulster to keep and divers felonies trespasses and other mis-deeds in our said County perpetrated to hear and determine assigned We being willing for certain causes to be certified as well of a certain plaint in our Court before you without our Writ between Henry Felt Plaintiff and Abel Gal Defendant of a plea of trespass upon the Case as it is said lately levied or affirmed as of the whole Record and Process of the same plaint thereupon depending Do command you that the Plaint aforesaid as also the Record and Process aforesaid as fully and ~~absolutely~~ intirely with all things touching the same as before you they reside by whatsoever name the Parties aforesaid are therein called you send before us at the City of New York on Saturday the *twenty* eighth day of April instant under your Seal distinctly and openly together with this Writ that We may cause to be further done thereupon what of right and according to the Law of our State we shall see right to be done   Witness Richard Morris Esquire Chief Justice at New York the nineteenth day of April in the eleventh year of our Independence—

B. Atty   McKesson

◆ ◆ ◆

CC. Rule for Lease, Entry, Ouster

Supreme Court, New York State, 1784
[Jackson ex dem. Leonard v. Stiles, Post,
NY Supreme Court, 1784 (Ms. LC)]

James Jackson against
John Stiles for one
Messuage or Tenement
with the Appurtenances
in the City of New York, on
the Domin of James Leonard

New York
to wit

It is ordered by the Court, by the assent of both parties, and their Attornies, that Anthony Post of the City of New York Carpenter, may be made Defendant, in the place of the now Defendant John Stiles, and shall immediately appear to the plaintiff's Action, and shall receive a Declaration in a plea of Tresspass and Ejectment of the Tenements in Question, and shall immediately plead thereto, not guilty; and, upon the Trial of the Issue, shall confess Lease, entry and ouster, and insist upon his Title only.—And if upon trial of the Issue, the said Anthony do not confess lease, entry and ouster, and by reason thereof the plaintiff cannot prosecute his writ, then the Taxation of Costs upon such Non pross. shall cease and the said Anthony shall pay such Costs to the plaintiff as by the Court of the people here shall be tax'd and adjudged for such his Default in nonperformance of this Rule; and Judgment shall be entered against the said John Stiles, now the causal Ejector by Default.— And it is further ordered that if upon the Trial of the said Issue a verdict shall be given for the Defendant, or if the plaintiff shall not prosecute his Writ, upon any other cause, than for not confessing lease, entry and ouster as aforesaid, then the Lessor of the plaintif[f] shall pay costs if the plaintiff himself doth not pay them.—

By the Court—

Hamilton for Plaintiff
Lewis for Defendant

SELECTED TITLES FROM **ALM PUBLISHING:**

Game, Set, Match: Winning the Negotiations Game
by Henry S. Kramer

The Essential Guide to the Best (and Worst) Legal Sites on the Web
by Robert J. Ambrogi, Esq.

On Trial: Lessons from a Lifetime in the Courtroom
by Henry G. Miller, Esq.

Inside/Outside: How Businesses Buy Legal Services
by Larry Smith

Arbitration: Essential Concepts
by Steven C. Bennett, Esq.

Courtroom Psychology and Trial Advocacy
by Richard C. Waites, J.D., Ph.D

Negotiating and Drafting Contract Boilerplate
by Tina L. Stark

Knowledge Management and the Smarter Lawyer
by Gretta Rusanow, Esq.

Also from AMERICAN LAWYER MEDIA:

LAW JOURNAL PRESS professional legal treatises—over 100 titles available

Legal newspapers and magazines—over 20 national and regional titles available, including:

The American Lawyer
The National Law Journal
New York Law Journal

Visit us at our online store:
www.lawcatalog.com